PRAISE FOR

The Grace in Grief

"Raw and vulnerable, *The Grace in Grief* reminds us both to give ourselves compassion during times of loss and to become our own fiercest advocate. For anyone who is struggling through miscarriage or infertility, this is a must-read. Not only does it normalize the very real trauma and grief that accompanies miscarriage, but it also emboldens women to take control of their reproductive wellness amid a healthcare system that systematically overlooks core fertility issues. Laura's storytelling is authentic, impassioned, relatable, and heartbreaking. It reminds us not to discredit any pieces of our story—and of the power that comes when we share our story with others."

—**JOHANNA MUTZ**, co-owner, laurelbox

"*The Grace in Grief* is a powerful and poignant reflection on the intensity of reproductive loss and how it impacts those affected. This stirring, beautiful book will no doubt provide solace for so many navigating the grief of pregnancy loss."

—**JESSICA ZUCKER**, PhD, and author of
I Had a Miscarriage: A Memoir, a Movement

"This raw, impassioned, and wise book should be required reading for anyone having experienced grief. Laura Fletcher brings compassion and grace as she shines a light on the reality of miscarriage. *The Grace in Grief* is bold and offers insight on an often broken medical system that is failing us. Without a hard look at reproductive medicine, we'll never change it—and that is exactly what Laura asks us to do."

—DR. ANDREA VIDALI, MD

"*The Grace in Grief* drew me in the second I started reading it, even though I personally know Laura and Clay's story inside and out, as I worked closely with her during her trying-to-conceive journey. The way in which their story is told, the way in which Laura shares her suffering and her process, is not only beautiful, but it will lift the pain and suffering for so many. Laura, as I always said, was one of my 'best students.' She taught me things as she learned them, and to see her turn her journey into her purpose is one of the most inspiring things I have ever seen. Wherever you are on your fertility journey, or if you are already through, or you have gone through this grief and it remains unprocessed, please take the time to dive into this book and allow yourself the space to find the grace in grief. And share it with others. Sharing lifts the shame."

—AIMEE RAUPP, MS, LAc, and author

THE
Grace IN Grief

THE
Grace IN Grief

HEALING AND HOPE AFTER MISCARRIAGE

Laura Fletcher

RIVER GROVE
BOOKS

This book is a memoir reflecting the author's present recollections of experiences over time. Its story and its words are the author's alone. Some details and characteristics may be changed, some events may be compressed, and some dialogue may be recreated.

Published by River Grove Books
Austin, TX
www.rivergrovebooks.com

Copyright © 2022 Laura Fletcher
All rights reserved.

Thank you for purchasing an authorized edition of this book and for complying with copyright law. No part of this book may be reproduced, stored in a retrieval system, or transmitted by any means, electronic, mechanical, photocopying, recording, or otherwise, without written permission from the copyright holder.

Distributed by River Grove Books

Design and composition by Greenleaf Book Group and Sheila Parr
Cover design by Greenleaf Book Group and Sheila Parr
Cover photo by Charles Clay Fletcher
Cover images © Shutterstock / Obsessively and Brita Seifert

Publisher's Cataloging-in-Publication data is available.

Print ISBN: 978-1-63299-614-5

eBook ISBN: 978-1-63299-615-2

First Edition

Dedicated to Jolene Ray and Isla Maris
Thank you for choosing me to be your mother.

Rosie,
I am rooting for you
♡
xoxo Laura

I HAVE LEARNED NOW THAT WHILE THOSE WHO SPEAK ABOUT LIFE'S MISERIES USUALLY HURT, THOSE WHO KEEP SILENT USUALLY HURT MORE.

—C. S. LEWIS

Contents

Introduction: To My Readers .1

PART I: SOMETHING IS WRONG WITH ME 3

1: How Do I Survive This—Again? 5

2: Wild and Wonderful Ride 11

3: Four Miscarriages in Five Years 23

4: Statute of Limitations 33

5: Iceland: Desolation and Hidden Beauty 41

6: Grief Is a Strange Thing 47

7: Common or Not, It's Just Not Normal 53

8: Not Losing Hope Despite a Grim Diagnosis 63

9: My Labs Confirm What My Heart Already Knew 67

10: Please Come, Please Stay 77

11: Finally, Another Birth Announcement 97

12: Nearing Delivery Under the Shadow of COVID-19 . . . 105

13: Isla 111

PART II: THIS IS WHAT SUPPORT LOOKS LIKE . . . 117

14: The Birth of Selah Fertility 119

15: Infertility: Colossal Crisis or
    Monumental Opportunity? 129

16: A Model for Supportive Medicine: The
    Endometriosis Summit 133

17: Knowledge and Grace 147

Gratitude and Acknowledgments 155

Reading and Resources 159

About the Author 163

INTRODUCTION

To My Readers

I would like to begin by sharing with you that this story is, by nature, a series of highly triggering events. I have no doubt that you have experienced trials, tribulations, and trauma. I know this because you and I are really one and the same. I share this warning because there have been many moments in my life that I wish came with a flashing, bold TRIGGER WARNING label.

Please know that my intention in sharing the details of these events is trifold: First, the process of writing my story has proven to be cathartic (I encourage it). Second, I hope to shine light on the reality of miscarriage, and, unfortunately, recurrent miscarriage. Third, I hope to help you find answers and overcome your struggles through tangible action and a mindfulness practice that I have come to know as the concept of *selah*.

PART I

Something Is Wrong with Me

CHAPTER 1

How Do I Survive This —Again?

THIS IS MY THIRD OF FOUR MISCARRIAGES.
IT'S THE MOST TRAUMATIC, BY FAR. IT'S
ALSO THE ONE THAT WAKES ME UP.

Grief is a strange thing; you're crumbling, everything is crumbling, but you're hyperaware. It's as if everything is magnified and you're shrinking.

I nod my head. Silence. In my ob-gyn's office, I am rational and quiet, composed. I can hear my doctor explaining that the fetus's heart has stopped beating. The "fetus." My baby . . . my fourth baby. The words seem to be flowing in slow motion. My husband, Clay, is arguing; insisting that we do another ultrasound. This can't be happening again. But it is and I know my doctor is speaking truth. I felt the void weeks ago but was too afraid to acknowledge it. Now it's slapping me in the face. It's exploding in my chest. It's seeping from me and drowning me.

Two days before, we were inhabiting an entirely different world: It's hot outside and I'm wearing tulle. Jolene is holding a red Solo cup against my tummy "listening" to her sibling. She's not cooperating and it's so damn humid. We're trying to capture the perfect photograph for our pregnancy announcement. It's January 2016 and I'm officially in my second trimester and ready to share the news publicly.

I'm frustrated and snapping at Clay for not getting the right angle. He's trying really hard but the lighting is terrible and my bump isn't prominent.

"Why didn't I just hire someone?" I mumble to myself.

I've only thrown up a couple times today, which is a vast improvement over the last three months. Actually, it's a vast improvement over the last two years. In the recesses of my mind, I hear a whisper: *What did you do?* Pushing that thought aside, I finally settle on a photo, and we announce that we're expecting: "Hello, lovely."

The next day, the cramping starts. I'm angry. I call my ob-gyn and frantically click through the automated options. The receptionist picks up—finally—and I explain the pain. I hear myself apologize for worrying and she connects me to the nurse. I remind the anonymous nurse that I've had two miscarriages and I apologize again. *Is she looking at my chart? She needs to reference my chart. Is this really me? Am I really apologizing?* The woman on the other end of the line tells me it sounds concerning and that I should come in for an ultrasound. I explain in a shrill tone that everything is fine; I heard the heartbeat last week.

CAN STRESS IMPACT THE OUTCOME OF A PREGNANCY OR NOT?

"173 beats per minute!" I say into the receiver. Silence.

"Babies with a heartbeat of 173 beats per minute don't just die," I shout.

After a long pause, she schedules my appointment for the next morning. She tells me to stay calm. She also tells me stress can't cause a miscarriage. I am confused. This type of contradictory messaging is rampant in fertility. Can stress impact the outcome of a pregnancy or not?

Twenty minutes later, I'm at dinner at a restaurant and my pants won't button. The waiter keeps offering me wine. *I don't want your goddamn house wine. Can't you see that I'm pregnant?* Our friends joke about the house wine while they sip their cocktails; I grind my teeth. I try to rationalize the cramping. *This can't be happening. It could be round ligament pain.* I put my game face on and power through dinner. I avoid the bathroom just in case I see something I can't un-see.

We're staying with my parents and it's a quick drive from the restaurant. We drive back in silence. I open my door before the car is even in park. I dash into the guest room and pull down my pants and underwear in one motion. Then I see it: the blood . . . my blood, her blood. I collapse in a puddle on the floor. As I fall, a revelation bursts from my lips: "Something is wrong with me!" I scream.

In the ob-gyn's office, I nod my head. I clench my jaw. I listen to the options. I want to die, but that's not included in the list of options. There are only three options: surgery, medication, or wait for my body to empty. Clay is still arguing about another ultrasound. He's in disbelief. I can't. I won't. I tell him in a whisper that there is no point, that our baby stopped growing several weeks ago. I'm already going over everything I did and didn't do. I shouldn't work so much. I should have forced myself to eat more; gotten a prenatal suppository. My ob-gyn reminds me that I know my options. Sadly, he's right and I feel my outrage bubbling. He says with a smile, "Next time, we'll make it stick." Tears slide down my cheeks and I agree to option two: a pill that will help pass the "byproducts of conception" in the "comfort" of my own home. This is a terrible decision, but I don't know that yet. We wait. We wait for nurses and instructions and medicine. We wait for sterile cups and consent forms. We drive across town for additional sterile cups and new instructions. We drive home and I'm suffocating. I am screaming inside my head: *How do I survive this—again?*

I NOD MY HEAD. I CLENCH MY JAW. I LISTEN TO THE OPTIONS. I WANT TO DIE, BUT THAT'S NOT INCLUDED IN THE LIST OF OPTIONS.

I climb up onto the huge bed in my parents' guest room. The faint smell of detergent makes my stomach turn as I bury my head into the pillows. The medication works almost immediately. I feel a feral and completely involuntary urge to get down on the floor like a dog and push. As the chaos begins, I recall a book I once read about a young, outcast girl that gave birth alone in a river. *How did she know what to do?* I wonder. I panic—this feels like labor. I can't do this. This isn't what was explained. This isn't what I expected. It occurs to me—and not for the first time—those expectations are hugely problematic.

The bleeding comes on in a flood. I feel completely wild—as though I'm no longer a human being. I'm simply surviving, reacting. I'm confused and terrified. I'm wearing a heavy-duty pad but quickly realize it's not sufficient. Clay helps me to the toilet and out of my underwear. And then the bomb drops. When I see her, I can't process what is happening. This was not supposed to happen. I was not supposed to recognize her. She was not supposed to be a baby. She was supposed to be tissues. I see her tiny black eyes starting to form and her arm buds. Her skin is completely translucent, like a jellyfish. I lose it. I'm hysterical and I can't breathe. I'm screaming and nobody can help me. I have brought this trauma on myself. The bleeding gets worse and I faint. As I regain consciousness, I hear my husband shouting and see my mom in the background wringing her hands. It's like she's looking right through me. Clay carries me to the bathtub. The scene in my wake looks like the site of a massacre. *Where is she?* I wonder. *Where is she?* I will wonder for the rest of my life.

When I gave birth to Jolene, I entered a different state of mind . . . a sort of temporary insanity that got me through labor. I'm here again, in this psychotic limbo. I'm aware that I'm out of my mind and I'm floating just above myself, watching the blood splatter onto the cream tile floor. I am a witness.

"Call an ambulance!" I overhear my ob-gyn demand over the phone. Clay is looking at me desperately. I can feel his fear. I refuse—partially because I want to die, partially because I don't want to put on pants, and partially because I no longer trust my ob-gyn. Even during this extreme chaos, I still manage to control something. Clay is collecting the "byproducts." He's storing her in a sterile cup. He's calling the doctor again and I'm listening. When he lifts me out of the bathtub, I catch a glimpse of myself in the mirror. I'm streaked with blood, my eyes are like a storm, and I'm broken. *Where is she?* I wonder again.

I bleed for days. Weeks. Months. I faint when I stand up. I have to be carried to and from the bathroom. When Clay goes back to work, I pee in a bucket next to my bed. I bleed into the bucket. I claw my way back into bed. I don't shower and I barely eat. I don't speak to anyone. I feel like I'm fading away.

This is my third of four miscarriages. It's the most traumatic, by far. It's also the one that wakes me up.

CHAPTER 2

Wild and Wonderful Ride

Sitting alone in the quiet of my apartment in 2011, I listen for the sound of Clay's Harley-Davidson. Being pregnant is the last thing on my mind. We barely plan our weekends, let alone our entire future. We work opposite shifts so the primary thing on my mind is just being able to spend time together. The sounds of his motorcycle fill me with both relief and excitement. Clay spends a lot of time fighting his demons and sometimes I'm not so sure he cares to. He likes to dance on the line, does Clay. The line between being unique and being wild. Sometimes he's a hippie and sometimes he's pure rock and roll. Other times he's an artist or an extreme athlete. I've seen him be many things, this man. We have big, dramatic fights and he encourages my tendency toward mania.

The next day, I wake up so nauseated I barely make it to the bathroom. When several more days of throwing up incessantly follow, I can no longer blame food poisoning from hibachi. My period is late. I'm twenty-five years old. I'm a vegetarian and I have no knowledge of prenatal care.

I call my gynecologist. He wants to see me right away. He performs an ultrasound and confirms the pregnancy. "You're about six weeks!" he beams. I squint at the black-and-white image on the screen. It reminds me of a tiny peanut floating in a black puddle. I'm in love.

At the time, Clay was working part time and partying full time. He was in no way prepared to be a father. He didn't react well at all to the positive pregnancy test. He disappeared and left me with nothing but my anxieties. It took a couple of weeks for him to process the shock, but he was with me for my next appointment with my new ob-gyn. We were surprised to be greeted by a very grumpy man who immediately told me I needed to start eating meat, then very casually stated that if I happened to miscarry, he wanted me to freeze the byproducts and bring them to him for analysis.

"Scoop as much tissue out of the toilet as you can, place everything in a Ziploc bag, and freeze everything. I'll need to test it," he said.

We sit and stare in disbelief. This thought never occurred to me as a possibility. *Why on earth would this man say such a thing?* Absolutely horrified, I left the office, never to return. I felt heartbroken and betrayed. I felt confused and angry. In hindsight I would wonder, *Did that awful man see something in me? Something I couldn't have known?*

Off to an intense start, the pregnancy got worse. My morning sickness turned into a severe case of hyperemesis gravidarum and I was throwing up on average twenty times a day. I would throw up when I woke up, on the drive to work, at work, on the drive home from work, and until I fell asleep. Sometimes, I'd wake in the middle of the night and throw up. I was miserable. In the first trimester, I lost almost twenty pounds. My medical team did nothing. "That's a sign of a healthy pregnancy!" they proclaimed. *Onward*, I thought.

I had to carry a bucket with me everywhere. It was much worse than the worst hangover I'd ever experienced. Worse than carsickness. Worse than the stomach flu. I continued to work as best I could but spent most of my day in the bathroom. I was in and out of the emergency room for IV drips. The doctors seemed indifferent, and I didn't know how to help myself. I couldn't hold down food or liquids. None of the traditional remedies helped and nobody ever offered me medication outside of the emergency room. At the time, I held the belief that no medication was safe during pregnancy and therefore didn't demand options. I was naïve. I was raised to believe that we power through all things. I didn't have the right approach to such a serious sickness. I just kept going.

My second trimester was great. The sickness subsided and I was glowing, just like everyone said I would. I had tons of energy and went into full nesting mode. At the time, Clay and I were living in a high-rise studio apartment downtown. The fire alarm would get pulled a couple of times a month and always in the middle of the night. After the fourth time, we decided it was time to move. With a baby on the way, it was the best decision for us. I paid the fine to terminate the lease early and we started packing. Thankfully, we didn't have a ton of furniture. The bulk of my possessions was clothing and most of the clothes felt ill-suited for my life moving forward. I doubted I'd need many sequined mini dresses or astronomically high heels in the near future.

We began looking for a house closer to my parents with plenty of rooms. By this time, Clay was besotted with our growing baby girl and had decided that he wanted six kids. I had negotiated down to two. My mom, beyond excited, happened upon a beautiful two-story home on about an acre of land. It needed a lot of love, but it was within our budget and in the area where we wanted to live. When we walked in for the viewing, we were greeted with walls in every imaginable color and the faint smell of marijuana. It was priced really well and we put in an offer. It was accepted.

"We want the home to go to a growing family," they said with kind eyes.

"Growing we are!" Clay laughed awkwardly, glancing at my belly as I held my breath.

We applied for a mortgage and got a phone call almost immediately. Clay's credit was questionable, and as a first-time buyer I wouldn't get approval alone.

"But I have excellent credit and a sufficient cash deposit," I argued.

"You'll need someone on the loan for approval," they responded.

We went to work and started digging through Clay's credit only to find the loan officer was right; it was a quagmire. When

Clay was fourteen, his father used his son's name to open a credit card account for himself. It had a significant balance on it.

"This is great news!" the loan officer said when we called him to explain. "All you have to do is prove that it's not your balance," he expanded.

The first response we got from Johnny, Clay's dad, was outright denial, followed shortly by placation. "Not a problem, brotha man!" he exclaimed. "I'll take care of it."

But he didn't. He stalled. For months. And our relationship suffered. Clay was angry and embarrassed. I was appalled and persistent. It was simple: if we wanted the house, Johnny had to fax the loan officer the statements showing that the payments were indeed coming from his checking account, not Clay's. The whole process should have taken twenty minutes. It took months and it damaged the trust between the Fletcher men forever. By the time the loan officer got the paperwork, I had been accused of fraud and escorted out of a bank (at seven months pregnant with my mother in tow) and Clay had said things he'll never forgive himself for. We got the house, but at a serious cost to our emotional well-being.

The closing date was just before the eight-month marker. We had painters and tile guys waiting for us when we pulled up with the keys. Everyone got to work immediately; we wanted to be in before Jolene was born. Jolene had different plans. Around the time I was escorted out of the bank, I went into preterm labor. I was in and out of the emergency room for the next six weeks. The nurses began to recognize me and all of them fell in love with Clay. The nurses always managed to keep things at bay and delay for a few days every time I came in, until they couldn't.

At thirty-five weeks, Jolene decided she was ready to see the world. I woke up to contraction pains, which by this point were normal. When I stood up, though, the mucus plug came away. Clay, wakened by my reaction, jumped up and turned into a full-blown tornado. He loaded up the car seat and hospital bag while barking orders.

"I need to eat," I reminded him.

"We can eat on the way," he said anxiously.

I agreed and we pulled in for a quick sandwich on the way to the hospital.

In the ER, they were unable to conclusively say if my water had broken. They ran two tests, which came back contradictory.

"We're going to admit you just to be safe," the nurse announced.

With a sigh of what I think was relief, Clay grasped my hand. As they wheeled me upstairs, I reminded him of the birth plan.

"Absolutely no drugs, Clay. I'm serious! Don't let them bully me. Don't let them give me a C-section either. The vaginal canal has imperative bacteria and it's necessary for the development of her immune system . . ." I went on and on. I had been doing some research.

When we got to the delivery floor, I was informed that my ob-gyn wasn't on shift. I felt a wave of anxiety wash over me.

"But she knows my birth plan! And she's on board with it. And, and, and . . ."

". . . and you'll be fine," Clay said.

Shortly after, the doctor came in and introduced herself. She was from the same practice, and I'd heard good things about her but had never met her before. A very high-energy woman, she rushed around the room and flew through the details of my chart. Her energy was making me nervous and the pain already had me on edge.

"Let's start Pitocin," she announced, snapping the chart closed.

"Am I in active labor?" I asked in shock.

"Pitocin will get things moving," she responded. "We're against the clock here."

Baffled, I declined. A few hours later she returned. This time, she insisted: "If we don't get Pitocin started, you're going to end up needing a C-section. Is that what you want?"

We went back and forth like this for several hours. Eventually, I caved as she pointed to the clock and explained that hospital policy deems a C-section necessary after twenty-four hours of labor due to "failure to progress." At that point I had been in labor for about fifteen hours. We were running out of time.

The nurse started the slow drip of Pitocin and I fell asleep highly irritated and disappointed in myself. Two hours later I woke up in shocking pain. In a panic, I called for Clay and asked him to help me get to the bathroom. When I stood up my water broke. "What the hell is happening?" I shouted. "I'll call the nurse," Clay stammered back.

I got to the bathroom with a trail of blood and fluids in my wake. As I started to come out of my sleepy fog, I realized that my water had broken and I was officially in active labor. *Freaking Pitocin*, I cursed.

The nurse was waiting for me when I got back to the bed.

"Let's check your cervix," she exclaimed. "Are you ready for an epidural yet?" she asked, peering up from between my knees. "No, I'm fine!" I stated, determined.

The contractions began coming hard and fast. They took my breath away. I climbed onto the birthing ball and tried to keep myself together. *You're fine, you can do this.* "Breathe!" Clay whispered.

I sat on the ball for hours, rocking. Back and forth, side to side. Breathe. The pain intensified and I felt myself starting to drift. The monitors started beeping and the nurses rushed in. "Let's get you on the bed," they half shouted.

The doctor walked in and said casually, "The baby's heart rate is fluctuating. She's in stress." *Oh my God.*

"What does that mean?" Clay demanded.

"It means we might need to perform an emergency C-section," she replied, annoyance thick in her voice. "You need to stay in bed; no more walking, no more ball," she ordered.

After that, the pain became unbearable. The nurse looked at me in disbelief as the contractions skyrocketed to the top of the monitor. "These are some of the most intense contractions I've seen," she said, "and I've been doing this for twenty years." Concerned, she added, "Only an hour left on the clock if you want that epidural." Furious, I asked her to leave. She smiled, squeezed my hand, and walked out without a word.

Twenty minutes later and twenty-three hours into labor, I changed my mind. "I need the epidural," I screamed.

"Are you sure?" Clay asked hesitantly.

"Now, Clay. Now!" I responded, a black cloud settling around my head.

The epidural was placed but the pain didn't subside. One leg went completely numb but I could feel everything else. Of course this would happen to me—what the hell.

"It's too late to fix it; we waited too long," the anesthesiologist explained apologetically.

I pushed for hours. Jolene was "sunny-side up," which means the back of her head was against the back of my pelvis and her face was pointed up toward my abdomen. This is referred to as "back labor" and it is horrifically painful. Bravo to the many women who have accomplished this without copious amounts of drugs. I applaud you. Also, I'm kind of scared of you.

Luckily for me, my regular ob-gyn came on shift at this point. She walked in, smiled at me, and said: "Let's have a baby!" *Hell yes! Let's do this, Dr. L.*

Jolene was totally stuck. I was exhausted and in an insane amount of pain. Plus, I pooped, and everyone lied to me about it.

"I can smell it," I said, mortified.

Clay, holding up my completely numb leg, tried to claim responsibility for the smell. He's a keeper.

"We're going to have to give her some help," my doctor said quietly to the nurses. Very discreetly, she grabbed the scissors, took hold of my perineum, and snipped it. Not once, but twice. Clay still has nightmares about me screaming in that moment. Epidural, my ass. But the episiotomy did the trick. Jolene just needed more room.

When they handed Jolene to me, I felt my entire life change. I felt no pain; I heard no noise. The world stopped turning. She was bright red and smooshed. She was long and smooth. Her skin was covered in a white, waxy film and her arms reached out in protest. Her little lips stretched over her gums and she struggled to open her swollen eyes. She was mine and she was perfect. Because she was five weeks early, the pediatric team rushed her to an intensive care unit where they could closely monitor her vitals. After holding her for what seemed like a second, they bundled her up and rushed her to another floor of the hospital. "Don't take your eyes off of her!" I screamed at Clay as he rushed out the door after her. The minute they left the room, I threw up all over myself. The drugs, adrenaline, and pain had taken their toll and I began to crumble. I was in shock. There was a lot of blood and my doctor reminded me that I had to pass the "afterbirth." I wonder, fleetingly, why I rarely hear anyone say "placenta." A few minutes later, she held up my placenta so I could see it. I've heard of people eating their placentas, and as I look at this massive, vascular organ, I shrink away. They discard it and begin sewing me up. In retrospect, I wish I'd shouted out "thank you!" to that incredible, life-sustaining organ, but it's not until much later that I'll understand its role. I fall asleep, and when I wake my parents are in the room. They look both immensely proud and incredibly worried. "I'm fine," I squeak.

> I CAN'T TAKE MY EYES OFF HER AND
> I SMILE ALL DAY WITH MY WHOLE
> FACE. IT'S TWO DAYS OF BLISS.

Finally, they wheel me up to our hospital suite where we stay for the next two days. Jolene and Clay are brought in and he assures me that he never left her side. *I know*, I think. *I know*. Jolene wears a little knit cap and is swaddled tightly in a blanket. I want to hold her every second of the day but I'm weak, so we take turns cuddling her and sleeping. The nurses come in hourly to check on us, and slowly the fog begins to lift. Sensation in my body returns. As my legs feel more stable, I get up and down repeatedly to stare at Jolene. I can't take my eyes off her and I smile all day with my whole face. It's two days of bliss.

When it comes time to leave the hospital, they let us know that Jolene will need to wear a portable "bili blanket" as she's dealing with some jaundice. So, we load up our newborn, her bili blanket, and all of her flowers and balloons. We're the happiest little family in the world but, as we pull onto the road, the anxiety kicks in. We've got to get this tiny, precious, helpless girl home. We have to navigate through downtown traffic and then commence a thirty-minute commute across town. I am very glad Clay is in the driver's seat. I sit in the back, glued to the car seat.

Our new home is nowhere near ready, so we settle in with my parents. I couldn't be more grateful, as this new mom thing is hard. We're up for feedings every two hours, another side effect of prematurity, and breastfeeding is not going very well. It's harder than I thought it would be, and I'm not sure who to ask for help. Jolene is sleepy and refuses to latch, so I begin walking a tight line of pumping, feeding, sterilizing, and sleeping. I'm a mess. I had made the assumption that because I had big breasts, breastfeeding would be easy. This assumption was based on zero evidence or research and now I'm very annoyed with myself. Clay makes lactation cookies, buys tinctures, and meekly mentions formula. I push on, torturing myself, for six weeks. When

I finally agree to give myself a break and try formula, I cry. I cry tears of guilt and relief. Motherhood becomes much easier after this transition. I get some sleep and Jolene seems satiated.

> LIFE IS WONDERFUL, AND A YEAR LATER, WE DECIDE WE'RE READY FOR ANOTHER BABY.

By the time our house is ready, we've settled into parenthood and feel comfortable in our new routines. I'm still on maternity leave, Clay is working on average forty hours a week, and Jolene no longer needs the bili blanket. We move in quickly and begin decorating. Life is wonderful, and a year later, we decide we're ready for another baby. I feel no fear, no trepidation, just sheer excitement.

CHAPTER 3

Four Miscarriages in Five Years

WE'VE ALREADY PICKED OUT NAMES AND A DOUBLE STROLLER. WE ARE BLISSFULLY NAÏVE ABOUT WHAT THE FUTURE HOLDS.

Over the next five years, every doctor I meet fails me. I miscarry four babies and I completely lose faith in myself, the medical system, and God.

Within a month of deciding we were ready for a second baby, I am pregnant. The nausea kicks in almost immediately. I knew I was pregnant before I confirmed it with an at-home test. Although hyperemesis gravidarum hits me hard, I am elated. We've already picked out names and a double stroller. We are blissfully naïve about what the future holds.

> I DID NOT KNOW THE RIGHT QUESTIONS TO ASK.
> I DID NOT KNOW WHICH TESTS TO DEMAND.

My second pregnancy ends quickly.

When I go in for my first ultrasound to confirm the pregnancy, I'm by myself and confident. To this point, the hCG beta tests measuring the "pregnancy hormone" look good. The numbers double as they should. However, the ultrasound tells a different story. No fetal pole or heartbeat is detected. The medical team uses terms like "blighted ovum" and "gestational sac." I stare at them blankly. I have never heard these terms and I'm not really sure what they're telling me. The doctor theorizes that perhaps we're doing the ultrasound too early and has me book a follow-up ultrasound. They don't run additional tests, they offer no support or advice; they simply send me home. I did not know the right questions to ask. I did not know which tests to demand.

> INSTEAD OF HONORING MY
> EMOTIONS, I JUDGED MYSELF.

About a year after Jolene was born, Clay started working in the oil industry. He works offshore and is gone, on average, eight months out of the year. This happens to be one of those months. I sit on my bed and flip through photographs of myself holding up a positive pregnancy test. I sent the pictures to Clay only a couple of weeks ago. I'm wearing a floral print dress and my hair is still damp. It's one of the last pictures of me before I knew the crushing pain my life would hold. I stare down at my smiling face, and I start to feel foolish. As the emotion bubbles up, I feel angry at myself for feeling foolish. Instead of honoring my emotions, I judged myself.

Soon after, the bleeding began. The cramping was mild—comparable to a monthly period. Had it not been for the hyperemesis and the early positive pregnancy test, I likely wouldn't have known I was pregnant. It would have seemed like a lingering stomach bug followed by a period.

When my doctor's office confirmed that the pregnancy wasn't viable, they explained that miscarriage is common and occurs often even after having a healthy pregnancy. The whole thing felt very scientific and clinical. I didn't feel a tremendous amount of sadness or distress. My reaction matched the tenor of the doctors. I was factual, rational, and calm. I believed them when they said, "This is totally normal."

After I re-dressed, the doctor came back in to answer whatever questions I had. The only one I could think of was "When can we try again?"

"Right away!" he responded. "You're perfectly healthy. No reason to wait." He seemed proud of himself and almost chuckled as he departed after sharing the news.

I get pregnant on my next cycle. I'm becoming attuned to the early signs of pregnancy in my body. My sense of smell becomes really heightened and I feel slightly dizzy. My mind feels a little foggy and I see black spots when I stand up too quickly. Shortly afterward, the vomiting starts. It comes on suddenly and intensely. Once again, I don't go anywhere without my bucket. I don't need to take a test, but I do. I watch the test strip closely as the lines begin to appear. First, they're faint, but as I hold my breath, they become dark and bold. I'm pregnant again, for the third time in as many years.

The sickness is absolutely crippling. I'm throwing up so often that I can't function at all. I'm in and out of the hospital for IV treatment and suppositories to stop the nausea and dehydration. It's not enough, it's never enough. Nothing works, the vomiting doesn't cease or even improve. I'm dropping weight and I can barely support myself. I spend most of my time in bed unable to hold down food or water. I'm unable to look after Jolene and I'm so grateful Clay is home. Although the hyperemesis is horrendous, I'm convinced it's a good sign. My doctor agrees that nausea means the baby is progressing and pumping hormones into my system. So I soldier on.

Preliminary blood work and ultrasounds all look "perfect." Although I feel physically wretched, I'm happy and excited. Clay and I tell our families the happy news and we truly believe everything is going well. We hear and see the heartbeat twice. Both times, the rate is strong and the doctor is encouraging.

But during an appointment in November of 2014, we hear the most devastating words parents can hear: "The baby's heart has stopped. There is no heartbeat." I stare at the screen and I can still see my baby. She's right there floating silently suspended in my womb. I can see her but all I can hear is the hum of the machine. It's dark except for the glow of the screen. Silence. It's such an intimate moment shared with a complete stranger. A moment in which everyone in the room changes forever. Like a tsunami triggered by a candle being extinguished across the globe.

The bleeding comes on its own. My doctor confirms via ultrasound that I've passed the "byproducts of conception." The lab tracks my hCG levels down to zero.

"You miscarried because you got pregnant too quickly after the last miscarriage," they explained when asked.

"You said it was safe," I squeaked back meekly, tears silently running down my cheeks.

I bleed for months. Nobody from the clinic checks on me. I think this is normal. Four months after my second miscarriage, I awake in a pool of blood. I'm staying with my parents because Clay is out of town again and I'm struggling to look after Jolene. I don't know how they knew, by somehow my parents were both in my room. Perhaps I yelled out for them. Perhaps I screamed. Either way, I end up in the hospital. Turns out, I had not passed the "byproducts of conception" and I needed an emergency surgery. The surgery is called "dilation and curettage" or "D&C." They dilate the cervix and use suction to clean out the womb. I had to fill out paperwork beforehand and noted that I wanted testing performed on the remains to try and determine the cause of the miscarriage.

Somehow, the hospital fails to follow these directions and all of the tissues are discarded. Weeks later, they attempt to pacify me by explaining that the "sample" would have been too degraded to test anyway. My heart breaks a little bit more. Logically, I know they're right, but to my heart that "sample" they discarded was my baby. Sacrificing these "tissues" in an effort to gain understanding and answers was one thing; sacrificing her to be discarded is another. I picture myself rummaging wildly through sealed containers of medical waste, searching for the baggy marked "Laura Fletcher" so that I can rescue her from that place and bury her somewhere peaceful. *Goodbye*, I whisper. *I'm sorry.*

༺༻

Most of my friends didn't know about the first miscarriage or the second. But the third—that one I allowed to change me—openly. I start admitting that I don't want to be strong. I don't want to be quiet or ashamed. Once I start talking, I learn that many of my friends have experienced a miscarriage and others struggle with infertility. I'm a reluctant member of a sisterhood; a sisterhood entrenched in grief. When I became a member of this 'hood, I was one in four. But with my third miscarriage, I'm an anomaly—an outlier. At university, I took a course on the statistics of psychology. When I enrolled, I was so excited to learn about the norms and abnormalities of the psyche. I was extremely disappointed when the mandatory course turned out to be on tracking and analyzing data as opposed to the actual data itself. Now, I wish I could track and analyze my own data. What do these figures really mean? How many of me are there? Expectations and disappointments . . . I sense a pattern here.

One morning not long after my third miscarriage, my mother, Jolene, and I board a flight bound for England to surprise my gran with a visit. At the airport, I realize I can't read the departure signs clearly. On the overnight flight, Jolene fades into sleep after the meal service. I'm in the middle seat wedged underneath the weight of her long legs. To my right, my mom sips red wine and remains focused on the small television in the back of the seat in front of her. I have to get up every couple of hours to change the diaper I'm wearing because I'm still bleeding heavily from the miscarriage. An airplane seat is uncomfortable at the best of times. Wearing an extremely bulky diaper makes it even worse. I wish my seat had an inflatable donut.

Seven hours later, we land in Manchester. Groggily, my mom drags our bags off the conveyor belt and we board a shuttle to get our rental car. I am frail so my mom won't let me lift anything. The weather is cold and gray. It's exactly what I need. Out of the harsh sun of Florida, I can breathe again and I seem to blend into the atmosphere here. I was born in Scotland and always feel slightly adrift elsewhere.

Unaccustomed to the car, my mom struggles with the first roundabout, but by the time she's on the highway, she's more comfortable. She scans the road signs looking for a Marks and Spencer Simply Food convenience stop. When she finds one, our spirits lift and we pull in for our favorite road-trip sandwiches: coldwater prawn and mayonnaise. Jolene opts for cocktail sausages and fruit. Back on the road, we're feeling quite at home again.

We arrive unannounced at my gran's house. We pull up as she's standing on the curb with her sister. She can't believe it's me and rushes to me shrieking. She looks at me like I'm a ghost and the concern is palpable. In hindsight, this was terribly selfish of me as she's too old for such surprises, but after my latest miscarriage all I want is to be with my gran.

    She gives me hot tea and bacon sandwiches with ketchup. She makes me stay on the couch and my family surrounds me. They don't know what to say so they stare at me. Then someone whispers, "You shouldn't try to have any more babies; you're killing yourself." With the first stone cast, they all chime in and agree. "You are blessed enough with Jolene!" they chirp. "What more could you want?" they venture.

    Suddenly, the bacon sandwiches aren't sitting so well, and the tea feels like acid in my throat. I know they mean well. I know they love me more than they love even themselves. I also know they're speaking aloud my greatest fears and it's very hard for me to hear. Perhaps they are right.

∾

I spend hours walking the coastline of South Shields, England. I sit in silence while my uncle, Keith, drives me to and from the water's edge. He waits patiently as I let the wind blow through my hair and ruffle the despair. The silence feels safe. We visit Tynemouth Priory, and I wander through 2,000 years of history. Despite the wild gusts coming off the North Sea, the air feels saturated with struggle. My mom is here too, holding Jolene's hand. She's in charge for now, a stand-in as I fall apart. Keith drove four hours to visit with us. He watches as I wander through the grounds trailing my fingers across the tombstones. We all take pause. It is here I start to reflect. I stop powering through.

"I know I can't do much but I had to be here," he said when he walked through the door at my gran's, not long after we arrived ourselves. At 6'4", Keith took up most of the hallway. *A giant in a cottage,* I thought—not sure how to tell him, "Thank you."

Four days later, he drives us back to Manchester. On the way, we detour to York. Although I'm from Scotland and frequent the UK, I hadn't been to York but felt a strong calling to the cathedral. It's pelting down rain and Keith barely fits in his own car with all of us piled in. Jolene's car seat takes up most of the backseat, my mom is wedged between the window and a mound of winter coats, and I'm up front still wearing a diaper under my jeans. When we arrive in York, we can't find parking. So Keith pulls up to a curb near the cathedral and we jump out into the puddled streets. The wind lashes my face and the rain feels cold against my skin. When I walk through the massive doors of the cathedral, I feel an immediate peace. The weather is keeping most people indoors so it's quiet and uncharacteristically empty. We sit in the back pews and listen as the organ chimes. The choir begins practicing and it's as if the entire event has been laid on for us. *God, can you hear me? I'm sorry.*

Jolene announces that she's hungry, so we walk out to a small café where Keith is waiting. After many laps around the winding, traffic-laden streets, he's found parking and we all sit down for tea, hot chocolate, and fruit tarts. I sip my tea and think to myself, *Perhaps I'll stay.*

As we board the flight back to Orlando, my heart breaks a tiny bit more. Breathe.

CHAPTER 4

Statute of Limitations

At a follow-up appointment with my ob-gyn back in Orlando, my doctor asks me when I'd be ready to give "it" another shot. I look at him through blurred eyes and burst into tears. Another shot? I tell him all I need from him is an anti-anxiety medication and something to knock me out. At this point, he thinks to ask how I'm doing. Apparently, he hasn't noticed my hands shaking, my unwashed hair, and my inability to hold a conversation or eye contact. Because miscarriages are normal, right? He puts me on a Zoloft-Xanax cocktail and hands me a three-page handout with counselor recommendations. He also tells me I should have my eyes checked but fails to mention that extreme trauma can cause permanent vision damage. Who knew? Anyway—where was this list two years ago? Two weeks ago? And have I truly lost the ability to determine that I need help without a printout? I chide myself as I was a psychology major, and I laugh out loud at the list in my hand. My doctor glances at me nervously through his peripheral vision. How did

I get here? I no longer recognize myself and I am disgusted. My subconscious loves to keep me in check; she's a bitch.

When I get home, I push the list aside and stare at my computer. I pick up my phone and reach out to one of my favorite professors from college and the lady that helped rescue my marriage after Clay's reaction to our first pregnancy.

Dr. Judi says she'd love to see me again. I'm in her chair the next day. When I arrive, I don't know what to say. I almost throw up walking into her office and I look at her in bewilderment. I still can't stop shaking and the Xanax hasn't quelled the panic attacks. She fights back tears and I fight myself. I stumble through my story by working backward. I choke over my words and entwine my fingers so tightly that I draw blood with my unkempt nails. Judi is patient and gentle. She asks how I feel and where the feeling resonates. I'm overwhelmed by a multitude of emotions but for today we acknowledge my anger. I'm past the denial stage and I'm outright furious. This anger is housed in my chest, compounded by a suffocating sadness in my throat. She asks me to breathe acceptance into these areas and emotions; she suggests that I let them speak.

"What do they want to say?" she asks.

I'm surprised. I don't want them to have a voice—I want them to go away. Surely, they're like weeds and will flourish if I water them. Something about this exercise feels phony, disingenuous. Judi continues to encourage me and rephrases her intention. I'm very uncomfortable and cannot open up. I meekly state that I simply want the feelings of anger and sadness to go away. I change the subject to my anxiety, which has taken a physical toll, and insist that I need a medication that still allows me to work. When she suggests that I take a medical leave, it's like a bolt of lightning to my chest. *Preposterous!* I think. My mouth is working before my brain as I ramble off an automated response about the house we're building and how busy I am. My heart sinks but I keep rambling. My fingernails pierce the flesh of my palms and my eyes dart nervously around the room for a clock. I reach for my cell phone—I probably have a million emails. I am needed, dammit!

As my hour comes to an end, Judi jots down the titles of a few books and we make a secondary appointment. She suggests I come back as soon as my schedule allows and tells me again how heartbroken she is over everything I've told her. When I get back to my car I scream and hit my steering wheel. I consider driving to the airport and jumping on the next plane to anywhere but the vibration of my cell phone jolts me back into reality. "Laura speaking."

What do you do when the person you were born to be isn't the person you become? When your identity is so entwined with an idea, it's hard to separate the two? Like most little girls, I played "house" when I was young. I was always the mother and my little brother, Adam, was always the dog. If only I'd always played the dog . . .

I HAVE TO GRIEVE THE LIFE I THOUGHT I'D HAVE
AND ACCEPT THE LIFE I ACTUALLY HAVE.

As a teenager, I was proud of my thick thighs, full breasts, and wide hips: mama material. I thought of myself as a mother long before I actually became one. Even my astrological sign touts motherhood as a central force. Virgo personified. So much of me identifies as a mother. And don't get me wrong, I am a mother. Just not the mother I thought I was going to be. We're not the family I envisioned myself having. My house isn't full the way I thought it would be. Our dinners are more intimate and less noisy. Our car has one car seat, not two. Jolene has outgrown her stroller before we ever have the need for a double stroller. I have to grieve the life I thought I'd have and accept the life I actually have.

Halloween is approaching. I hate Halloween, always have. But now, it's different. The holiday marks a miscarriage for me. It's also a harsh reminder that Jolene doesn't have any siblings to trick-or-treat with. I wish Clay were home so I could pawn off the festivities and curl up in bed. He's in Africa and I don't have to work, so it looks like I need to figure out a costume.

My phone rings. It's my could-be lawyer's assistant. She's reminding me of the medical "statute of limitations." Do I want to move forward? I mumble something about waiting on test results and tell her I'll call her back, again. I'm not waiting for results. I haven't even taken the tests. In fact, I "lost" the paperwork listing the tests I need to get done.

When I update Clay over the phone, he says, "Hmm... that's unlike you."

No shit.

After the third miscarriage, a friend pointed out that the medical staff at my ob-gyn's office had failed me. "I know," I replied apathetically.

But as I ruminated over my friend's words over the next few weeks, I became angry. Very angry. I called Judi and set up an appointment. "I feel like I need to do something," I stated, sitting on the edge of her couch cushion. "They can't get away with this!"

"What do you want to do about it?" asked Judi cautiously.

"Should I sue them?" I pondered out loud.

"You certainly have a case. What they did is awful," she nodded sympathetically.

I start listing the timeline and going over the details, a stream of pain and disbelief.

"It is awful," I agree.

When I called a lawyer to discuss suing, he was horrified by my experiences.

"What doctor is this?" he demands to know over the phone. "I've never heard anything like this before. What do you mean they didn't run the tests on you?"

"They just kept telling me I was fine," I responded. "After the ultrasound, they said everything was clear but it wasn't. I still had byproducts, and I almost bled out as a result. I woke up in a pool of my own blood," I explained.

> I NEEDED TO FORGIVE MYSELF AND MOVE FORWARD, SO THAT'S WHAT I DID.

"How could they miss that?" he asked incredulously. "You definitely have a case, Laura," he stated.

But as the weeks went by, I pictured myself on the witness stand. I pictured my parents in the courtroom and I felt all of the pain that would be laid out for everyone to see. In the end, I decided to focus on the future, not the past, so I dropped the idea of a lawsuit. I needed to forgive myself and move forward, so that's what I did.

※

After giving up the idea of a lawsuit, Clay and I decide to focus on healing. He uses words like spa, meditation, yoga, and reconnecting. The reconnecting piece is important to us because we became parents before we became husband and wife. We've spent the last seven years being pregnant, parents, and new homeowners (x2). We've experienced every emotion under the sun and have become closer at times than ever before but also extremely cautious and strained. We're both exhausted in every sense of the word. We're fighters, Clay and I; we fight for each other, with each other, and about each other. I see you, double-edged sword.

Because I have been so entrenched in grief, I haven't been in a space where I could engage in healing or connection with Clay. During these times, I am awake for days walking through life like a zombie. I am joyless and full of despair. Eventually, I become numb and that scares me even more. If I can't feel the anxiety, is it gone? If I'm not sad, am I heartless? Exhaustion throws me into autopilot and I beat on against the current.

While navigating this grief, I am often reminded of Fitzgerald's Gatsby. A man who never lets go of the past—loving what was lost to him years ago and formulating his entire existence around it. Even when confronted with reality, he simply cannot accept it; he cannot let go. Once a Daisy figure, I have surely become Jay Gatsby—"borne back ceaselessly into the past." I am ever unable to be present and ever unable to relinquish my expectations.

The disappointment does not take away from the love I feel for my family. There are so many wonderful things about having a single child, and I remind myself of these things daily. When I dive into the reasons for having another child, it's hard to be honest. The most glaring reason is that I have an extreme fear of Jolene being alone. Being alone TERRIFIES me and therefore it terrifies me for her. What happens when I die? Who will she have? What if she never gets married on top of never having a sibling? The questions are endless. The shame is endless.

Recently, a friend told me that wanting your first child to have a sibling isn't enough justification for having a second child. I think if it was possible to view your life from an outside perspective, I *might* be able to look at this objectively. But as a mother, I seem to make the majority of my decisions to better my living daughter's life. Is this wrong? Wanting another child is biologically driven for me, it's a yearning. We are financially stable, we can provide a wonderful life, and we are full of love. But there's also a void. I wonder, would I want another child if I hadn't lost four? Am I simply competing? Trying to prove something? Am I trying to fill the crater that is eroding my soul? Yes, I've become dramatic in my grief. I embrace it and occasionally laugh about it. Silver linings.

For months after my miscarriage, I avoided sex. The thought of another pregnancy completely paralyzes me. Sometimes I wake up in the middle of the night and I can't breathe; I disintegrate into a full-blown panic attack because pregnancy is a monthly possibility when you're as fertile as I am.

My heart and my brain launch into a war: wants versus needs. I want to be pregnant but I need to figure out why I can't stay pregnant. Once the war starts, it's an avalanche, and everything I've done or thought over the last few weeks comes crashing down. Did you feel nauseated this morning? Could the condom have failed? When was ovulation? Why didn't you schedule the damn tests? And then, there it is: the little whisper that becomes a scream: *Do you want another child?* I can't breathe. I scramble for my Xanax but I'm out. I flip on the light and Clay jolts up in bed, reaching for the essential oils automatically. He douses me with lavender and glances at me timidly. He doesn't know what to say so he hands me some water and waits. Slowly, he begins to assure me that I'm not pregnant. I glare at him, and my mind starts launching an assault: *Does he want another child? How would he know if I'm pregnant? Does he not want me to be pregnant? How dare he.* We're never having sex again.

Each miscarriage takes a toll. On me. On Clay. On our marriage. We do our best to shield Jolene from the grief, the uncertainty, the arguments, and the anger. We're at each other's throats a lot. We bicker over everything and Clay walks on eggshells around me. My temper is unpredictable, and my fuse is almost nonexistent. We love each so much. We know we have a lot of work to do.

CHAPTER 5

Iceland: Desolation and Hidden Beauty

My brother is getting married. The wedding is in Iceland. I'm a bridesmaid and the dress is a full-length navy sequined number. Normally, I would be a size 4 in a dress like this; however, I order a size 8 because my body is still swollen after the last miscarriage. When it arrives and I slide it over my body, I look three months pregnant. I think part of my body physically hasn't accepted the loss. It's still holding onto something that will never be. My stomach protrudes and my back arches. My feet are swollen and my veins are visible through my skin. I have so much physical inflammation, it is as if every cell is in protest.

We pack our suitcase for three. Clay manages to get all of the sweaters, jackets, and wedding attire into one bag and I'm grateful for the ease this affords. Jolene is old enough to not require as much in-flight entertainment, snacks, or changes of clothing but we still pack it all just in case. We arrive to the airport in Hunter boots and leggings. Thankfully, we owned most of this attire so we didn't have to spend a ton of money on winter accessories.

When we land in Iceland, it's cold, gray, and wet. I'm grateful for our rain boots. Our rental car company is off-site so we take a shuttle to the location. We shuffle through the drizzle with our suitcase, backpacks, and the car seat. Jolene is grumpy and tired after the flight. It's not until we're in our rental car that I look around me. The land is torched and all I can think is "barren." We drive to the capital city, Reykjavik, and I'm pleasantly surprised by the colorful buildings. Our Airbnb is spacious and bright. Jolene makes herself instantly at home. She loves having everyone together in one place.

We venture out beyond the city. We have a large van so everyone piles in. There are large greenhouses throughout the country because nothing edible grows in the soil here. There is no abundance beyond the sea. It's a not-so-subtle reflection of how I feel. It's hard for me to focus on the festivities. Although I'm surrounded by family, I feel completely alone. My emotions are all over the place and my mood swings from manic anger to intense sadness.

The earth here creaks and groans. Heat bubbles up and cracks the ground. We drive for miles and everything looks and feels bleak. There are moors of boggy moss that stretch for miles. There are cliffs that seemingly jut out of nowhere and beaches covered in black sand. There are glaciers cascading over hills into deep, frozen valleys.

It's telling that even a place can be triggering to the grief brought on by miscarriage. Even a country entirely new to me with no emotional connection. No specific traumatic event occurred here for me but still, I'm affected. I wonder briefly if there is a collective grief here in Iceland, something lingering in the air centuries after some great loss. I'll look it up one day but not today. Not now.

As I continue to brood in this fashion, we pull up to a waterfall: Skógafoss. I am instantly bowled over. The sheer magnitude in and of itself is breathtaking but that's not what I notice. There are rainbows everywhere. Hundreds of them in every direction. The rainbow is a symbol for a baby born after miscarriage, stillbirth, or infant death. As we walk toward the thundering water, we're actually walking through rainbows. The damp clings to every inch of me. I'm drenched in seconds. This becomes a metaphor for my entire experience of fertility, miscarriage, recurrent miscarriage, secondary infertility, and the relentless hope that beckons me to try again. In this place which, until this very moment, has felt raw and scary and desolate, suddenly I am immersed in beauty so powerful that I am lost for words. Clay and I stand next to each other bewildered. I look back on a photograph snapped of us in that moment and I can feel everything all at once. We were pushing through serious, life-altering darkness. Heartbroken, angry, scared, confused, disappointed, exhausted, and full of grief. But when I look at the photo, it's clear: Isla, our rainbow baby, was always with us. She just knew I had a lot to learn. This is selah.

> *But, when I look at the photo, it's clear: Isla, our rainbow baby, was always with us. She just knew I had a lot to learn. This is selah.*

A few days later, we're standing in front of another waterfall waiting for the ceremony to begin. We're not as close to the water but I can still see rainbows dancing in the distance. The image helps to ground me as I focus my attention toward the reason I'm actually here: a union of lives. The wind is wild as Jolene comes up over the berm to the flat ground where the ceremony arch has been secured with boulders. Clay and I walk ahead of her to take our places up front. Jolene is the flower girl but when I glance back at her I know she's changed her mind. She stands frozen grasping her basket and shouts out for us. As we jog back toward her, she almost bursts into tears.

"I'm too cold!" she squeaks.

With that, Clay swoops in and becomes both groomsman and flower girl. I'm reminded of how naturally he has fit into his role as a father. He seems so at ease with Jolene. Instantly, she feels more comfortable and the procession continues without another hitch.

Adam wears a kilt and has a thistle pinned to his lapel. I feel pride bubble up in me as he walks into his future while still honoring his past. The two can coexist. We can step bravely into the unknown. Lexi, my very soon-to-be sister-in-law, has wisely thought ahead and provided tartan blankets for the guests. As I look across the crowd, I see a smattering of family and close friends all wrapped in the same tartan Clay wore at our wedding. The moment feels cyclical and safe. Like an ah-ha moment I once had years ago watching the tide roll in and then back out. Ever changing, ever the same.

In retrospect, Iceland is a desolate place. A place where you can't hide from your grief because it is reflected back at you in the very landscape. It feels heavy and dramatic and it's completely wide open. It would be easy to settle here and slowly nurse away the pain, tucked away in a remote place with a roaring fire and the eerie sound of nothing. But it's also a place of hidden beauty and revelation. A place that feels so deeply rooted in the past but also is paving the way for a different future. It's quite inspirational, really. It says to me, quietly: "You can retract and continue to grow in the dark. You have time. You do not always need to be stretched to the limit, straining. You do not always need to plan and prepare. You can simply be." *Selah*.

> *You can retract and continue to grow in the dark. You have time. You do not always need to be stretched to the limit, straining. You do not always need to plan and prepare. You can simply be.*

CHAPTER 6

Grief Is a Strange Thing

Christmas. It's here, again. Everyone is excited and buzzing. Jolene has revised her list to Santa at least five times and is on a daily countdown. I'm fighting to be present and joyful but I cannot stop thinking about last Christmas. I was malnourished and dehydrated then, fighting to stay alive and keep my baby alive. I survived but failed in my most urgent war. I find myself wishing the results were reversed. Simultaneously, I'm incredibly angry with myself for even thinking this way. My mind is spinning and I hear so many voices telling me, "You need to focus on what you have and be happy with it. You're so blessed." The rage bubbles up.

I decide it's okay to spend Christmas in my pj's. For some reason, I've offered to host Christmas this year. Why? Because I'm an overachiever that drowns myself in tasks so I don't have time to hear the pain. Turkey, anyone?

After the Christmas holidays, I return to work. I'm scrolling through Facebook and see another pregnancy announcement.

It's an acquaintance of mine announcing her third pregnancy at six weeks. I'm shocked. A six-week announcement? Who does that? I'm at work and I become so overwhelmed with emotions that I almost bring on a panic attack. I'm angry, jealous, sad, and scared for her. I take the announcement personally, knowing how irrational I'm being. Will these emotions ever go away? I am not this ugly, judgmental girl.

My last miscarriage was my fourth. Another baby girl, another heartbeat extinguished within me.

My fourth miscarriage occurs under the care of a reproductive endocrinologist, the "best" in the state. Under his watch, I've been getting weekly injections of progesterone oil, regular ultrasounds, and lots of attention. However, it doesn't prevent the destruction.

For weeks, Clay and my dad have had to pin me down and give me the intramuscular progesterone injections in my buttocks. It takes me hours to prepare for each shot. We employ all of the tricks—warming up the oil, icing down my butt cheek. Nothing makes it easier. The oil is thick. I feel it flooding the muscle. I develop hard welts in my muscle and wince every time I have to sit down.

At eight weeks, while in the exam room at my new ob-gyn's office, I explain that I feel like something is wrong. I have lower back pain and that's never a good sign for me. The doctor insists everything is fine and proceeds to discuss my birth plan. After twenty minutes, I lose my temper. She agrees to check for a heartbeat with a fetal Doppler. She switches on the machine and presses it against my stomach, all the while insisting everything is fine and I'm just paranoid. After a few moments of silence, I can feel her anxiety building and she too becomes quiet. She moves the Doppler back and forth in an increasingly frantic way and her brow begins to knit. In a panicked tone, she announces that it's too early for the Doppler to be accurate anyway and asks me to follow her to the ultrasound room. While walking to the room, she fills the awkward silence by muttering that the technician isn't in but she knows how to operate the instrument. Once in the dark room, I undress slowly, if only to delay the inevitable. My breathing becomes faint and I can feel my blood pressure dropping.

> I ADD THIS ROOM TO A LONG LIST OF OTHER ROOMS TAINTED BY LOSS AND HEARTBREAK.

Just before my appointment, my mom called me to say she'd join me. Now, she sits in the dark corner shrinking into herself. When they confirm that the heart has stopped, she lets out a tiny whimper and grasps for my hand. I pull away. I tell everyone to get out of the room and leave me be. I scream at them. As the door closes with an almost inaudible click, I let my eyes fall shut. I lie on the bed, my feet still in the stirrups, knees pulled together tightly as if in an attempt to hold everything in. I lie there in the dark and I listen to the hum of the ultrasound machine. I glance over at the screen, frozen on an image of my uterus and my baby. I know this is the last time I'll see her and I don't know if I should stare for hours or look away and flee from the room. I add this room to a long list of other rooms tainted by loss and heartbreak.

I slide my feet out of the stirrups and rock myself forward until they land on the step below the bed. I sit for a moment, wondering when the bleeding will begin. I stand up and get dressed. I prepare myself for the conversation I know awaits me on the other side of the door. I prepare myself to shield others from my pain. I steel myself, bracing for the pity.

When I emerge from the room, I speak first. I'm done letting her run the show. I explain to the doctor that I'd like to schedule a D&C as soon as possible. I feel possessed by death. My womb feels toxic. The surgery is scheduled for the following day. My mother and I take the elevator to my car. My mom stands next to me, terrified to speak but desperate to comfort me. I have no doubt that she's already called my dad for help. Clay is offshore and Jolene is at school.

We're in separate cars. I climb into mine and slam the door. Once inside, I drop my shield and I beat my steering wheel so hard I'm surprised the airbag doesn't deploy. I scream and scream and scream.

My mom stands beside the car, desperately trying to find a way to help me. I can see her moving toward the car then backing away over and over. She's trying to determine if I need space more than I need comfort. In the moment, she's right to back away. I am wild with anger. I am explosive. By the time my dad and brother arrive, I have bruised my hands and worn myself out with hysteria. I'm placid as I slide out of the driver's seat and into the passenger seat. My dad looks broken as he softly places his hand on mine. There are no words for the grief entrenching me.

"You'll be okay," he whispers.

"Will I?" I mouth back, no sound passing my lips.

The following day, I'm at the hospital for an emergency D&C. When my doctor walks into the room, I resist the urge to chide her. I resist unloading on her and think to myself: *You told me everything was fine. How could you do that?* I am so disappointed.

When the test results come back, they crush me like a boulder: trisomy 21—Down syndrome. This news makes my angel girl more real; it adds to her identity and the life she never got to live. So many people tell me it's a blessing that she didn't have to live that life. They say things like: "Well, maybe it was for the best." Each comment, each remark, each opinion strips me and I feel exposed, naked, alone. *Please, Lord, give me back my baby girl. Give me the chance to give her the best life possible. Let me show her how much I love her.*

After my fourth miscarriage, the one that was never supposed to happen because I was being given progesterone injections, I wasn't sure if I could ever try to conceive again. I was a shell of myself and struggled to identify with who I was and how the heck I could ever get back to where I was on the day I gave birth to Jolene. But I knew I had to because of how much I love her. She was everything to me in the deepest moments of despair; my only shining light.

CHAPTER 7

Common or Not, It's Just Not Normal

After my fourth miscarriage, I join an online support group for recurrent pregnancy loss. At first, being in the group is overwhelming. Women from all over the world are in it. Many share their stories and I'm all at once elated and devastated that so many of us exist. I'm not alone and this looks a heck of a lot like an epidemic. *Why are so many women losing so many babies?* I notice a trend within the group: a hero doctor that several women swear by. I didn't actively participate in the group—I just read posts—until one day I build up enough courage to share. Almost immediately, the "hero doctor" is recommended by a woman named Karen Nitzsche. I Google the recommended doctor. His website pops up and I click frantically through his site. The information is endless and so much of it pertains to the prevention of miscarriage. I can't believe it. He offers free consults over the phone, and I decide to schedule one. The receptionist explains his first availability for a consult is six weeks out.

"Six weeks?" I repeat in disbelief.

She confirms that I heard correctly and asks abruptly if I want to schedule it. She has no time for dillydallying, this woman has women to help.

"Yes," I stammer.

The next six weeks crawl by. I'm so anxious for my consult. I check the appointment in my calendar daily to make sure I have a reminder alarm set. I read through all of Dr. Jeffrey Braverman's blog posts and practically memorize the landing page of his website. I scour the internet for patient testimonials.

Dr. Braverman calls me an hour earlier than our scheduled appointment. I pick up my phone at work and rush outside to take the call. As he already had my file, he asked me a couple of questions about the miscarriages and, specifically, the heartbeats. He then says to me, as a matter of fact: "You have endometriosis. Silent endometriosis."

"Oh," I responded, dumbfounded. He is so direct. It's refreshing.

"Have you ever been checked?" he asked.

When I told him that I hadn't been tested despite asking many times, he launched into an assault: "What the hell is wrong with doctors? Where do you live? Florida? I can't believe these doctors. Ob-gyns don't know what to do with cases like you. I try to tell them, but they just won't listen!"

After he regained his composure, he said simply: "I need you to come up to New York. Trust me, you have endometriosis, and I can help you."

"HOW DID ALL OF THESE IDIOTS MISS THIS?"

And so, I booked a flight. His promise was irresistible. His passion was contagious.

───※───

Clay and I landed at JFK airport on a cold, overcast day in March. We checked into our modern hotel on the Lower East Side and walked around the corner to a sushi restaurant that was closing soon. It was our first date in far too long, and we sat staring at each other over gluten-free soy sauce, bewildered by the week ahead.

I was advised to eat a heavy breakfast in preparation for my appointment the following day, as it would include a twenty-nine-vial blood draw. As someone who is petrified of needles, this was extremely daunting to me.

The next morning it's very wintry as Clay and I walk past Central Park, bagels in hand, toward the Metropolitan Museum of Art. We know the city well and, in this moment, it felt like we could be residents. Not here for Broadway, the parks, or the restaurants—we were here to meet with doctors. We didn't have the luxury of strolling through the park but instead had to stick to the sidewalk. The energy was different. We didn't stay up late last night soaking in as much as we could. We retired early and set our alarms. I couldn't tell if the overriding feeling was excitement or anxiety, but with each block I could feel my nerves heightening.

When we walked into the office, I was surprised. The Hero was humble in his dwelling. No self-portraits lined the walls and he didn't have his stats scrolling across an obnoxiously large TV: a nice reprieve, I must admit. Dr. Braverman bustled to and fro while his nurse called people back to start diagnostics. I sipped my kombucha and forced my mind to slow down. We sat for ages watching the scene. I'm notoriously early for appointments and doctors are generally running behind. I sit in silence bracing myself for the questions. The ones they all ask: "How many times have you been pregnant?" "When was your last menstrual period?" When they call my name, I swallow hard and clench my jaw. Clay smirks at me and the nurse escorts us into a room and quickly gets started. I'm sweating before she even places the needle. A dizzying 20 minutes later, she hands me a chocolate lollipop and ushers us into Dr. Braverman's office leaving tubes of myself behind. What we found was a man surrounded by books and diligently at work. He was entirely engrossed, in fact. Perhaps this could be my hero after all, a man after my own heart. I don't know it now, but I'll envision this room for the rest of my life.

With a hurried "Hello," Dr. Braverman went over my history in detail. He was angry, very angry. His anger was encouraging, empowering even.

"I wish I could say this type of thing is rare," he said, jaw tense.

I scoot to the edge of my chair and lean forward.

"But common or not, it's just not normal. It's just not okay!" he ejaculated (I love a good fertility pun).

I sat completely transfixed, wondering how many times he'd had this same conversation with a woman just like me, a woman who thought she was alone. Grasping for answers and hoping for a solution.

Suddenly he turned sad, perhaps to match my sentiment. He told us how, as a young medical student, he realized that nobody was helping women stay pregnant and then he told us about the sleepless nights that followed. He was determined to help.

> "YOU'RE USED TO PAIN," HE RESPONDS. THIS HITS ME HARD. IT HAD NEVER OCCURRED TO ME BEFORE.

"The money is in the getting of women pregnant but not the keeping of women pregnant," he seethed. IVF quickly came under the gun, followed shortly by the entire profession of reproductive endocrinologists. He expanded on his frustrations with the medical community and complex fertility cases, stating fact after fact and citing case over case. He rubbed his face. In that moment I knew he would help me. The next step, he insisted, was surgery to excise the endometriosis he was convinced I had.

"Your mother had it. Let's do an ultrasound and see what's going on," he said.

"I don't experience a ton of pain with my period," I say.

"You're used to pain," he responds.

This hits me hard. It had never occurred to me before.

Ultrasounds are a trigger for me; they send me to a place that looks very much like post-traumatic stress disorder.

"Okay," I mumble, my blood pressure dropping.

The ultrasound is quick and painful.

Dr. Braverman watches my face contort and says, "It shouldn't be so painful. Something is going on with your cervix and your ovaries are lit up with cysts. We have to consider PCOS as well as endometriosis."

"Oh," I say again, lightheaded and dumbfounded to hear him mention polycystic ovary syndrome.

"How did all of these idiots miss this?" he says, clearly speaking to himself.

He calls his nurse in. "Look at this!" he says indignantly, pointing at the black spots on my ovaries.

"Clearly polycystic," she responds.

He removes the ultrasound wand, looks at me with compassion, and asks me to rejoin him in his office when I'm ready.

> I CAN'T EXPRESS THE AMOUNT OF VALIDATION AND HOPE I FEEL IN THIS MOMENT.

He rushes out of the room, and I'm left feeling very nauseated in a paper gown. Clay hands me a baby wipe and waits for me to speak. "What the heck?" is all I can muster.

The following day, we meet with Dr. Andrea Vidali, the surgeon, for another ultrasound. He concurs with Dr. Braverman. "Surgery is a must," he concludes.

He knits his brow and exhales deeply through his nose. For a moment it's like he's alone in the room. When he comes back to us, he looks at me and says very calmly, "Don't worry, we can help you."

I can't express the amount of validation and hope I feel in this moment. Dr. Braverman and Dr. Vidali were listening to me. They were actually listening. They had both taken the time to read the pages and pages of my medical file. Not only were they listening, but they were actively pursuing a solution. They both spent a tremendous amount of time answering my questions. I feel immensely supported. They talk to me about the impact of endometriosis on egg quality and fertility. They explain that it causes a high level of inflammation in the body, and they have no doubt it's a factor in my recurrent miscarriages. They talk about symptoms of endometriosis that I've never considered. Things like fatigue, bloating, headaches, and referred pain.

"So it's not just bad cramps?" I ask.

"Many women don't experience bad cramping and yet we find substantial endometriosis," he responds. "Endometriosis is not widely understood, and a lot of the accessible information is actually very inaccurate."

We agree to move forward and confirm surgery in New Jersey in two days' time.

Surgery requires bowel prep, which is a polite way of describing intentionally giving yourself diarrhea for at least 12 hours. In fact, diarrhea is an understatement. Unfortunately for Clay, I had to "bowel prep" in a New York City hotel room the size of my home closet without a door separating the sleeping area from the bathroom. True love is waiting in that room in case your wife needs water and can't get off the toilet for long enough to walk the five steps required to get a refill. It's a very long night for both of us.

The next morning, we loaded our suitcases into our Uber and headed over the bridge to New Jersey. We pulled up to the W hotel, checked in, dropped off our bags, and walked the couple of blocks to the hospital. Dr. Vidali asked me to arrive at 10:00 a.m. but in true type A fashion I arrived early in hopes we'd get the show on the road. We waited for hours as the nurses took blood, placed IVs, and offered assurance that I was in the right place.

"Your surgeon is the best," they chanted, showing me pictures on their phones of new mothers holding their miracle babies. Their voices rang through the empty halls, "My niece's friend's sister, Janice, got her rainbow baby!" I lay there trying desperately to distract myself from the two IVs protruding from my hands until finally the anesthesiologist arrives—the unsung heroes of my last six years. I perk up immediately, as this means the surgery is near but more importantly, the sweet oblivion of sleep without nightmares. Sleep without the interruption of a panic attack. I am aware of this attraction and remind myself to be careful because it's very glaring that in another life, I could have been a drug addict.

They wheel me through the locked double doors and Clay stands pressed against the glass watching me go. When the elevator doors slide open to reveal the sterile surgery, I begin to feel nervous. Am I about to get an exploratory surgery I may not need? What the hell am I doing? How did I get here? But then, Dr. Vidali is by my side. He is so confident and warm that it's easy to relax around him. He introduces me to everyone in the room. They're like a family and that, too, feels reassuring. *This is their norm*, I think to myself. *Surgery is what they do.*

"What if you don't find anything?" I ask out loud.

"Then we'll know. But I wouldn't have you in this room if I wasn't convinced," he responds.

When I wake up, they ask me if I have to urinate. I do, but then the nurse explains I have to fill up a jug to a certain point before I can be released. I'm sure I can manage that, as I feel as though I could explode. Nope, I was painfully short. For the next six hours I alternate between sleep and sipping ginger ale. I am so incredibly groggy. I took forever to fully wake up and even longer to pass the pee test.

When we get back to the hotel, hotel staff are waiting with a wheelchair. I rolled into our suite overlooking the river. It was dark but Manhattan was glowing. Through blurry vision, I watched the lights fade out as I drifted into a drug-induced sleep. Dare I dream that things were finally changing?

Dr. Braverman and Dr. Vidali were right. I had a severe case of endometriosis and polycystic ovary syndrome. My organs were "glued" together. As I sat in my hotel room overlooking the Hudson River, I cried. I cried for all the times I'd been dismissed and all the times doctors had overlooked my symptoms. I cried and felt a sense of validation. Perhaps now we'd have a successful pregnancy.

Flowers arrive from my friend, Jenn, and Clay goes on the hunt for the best gluten-free pizza. I move slowly from the bed to the window seat. I have to use hot towels on my shoulders and

I'm scared to cough. During the surgery gas was used to expand my abdomen. It travels to my shoulders as it works its way out of my body, and this discomfort is greater than the incisions. By this point, Clay understands how I recover from trauma. He keeps what I call "close distance." Always close enough in case I need him but never too close that I feel smothered.

During the second night of recovery, the guests in the room next to us throw a party. They are loud and young and so alive—and I hate them. After several calls to the front desk, the party raged on and I considered wheeling myself over in my chair. Maybe I'd raise hell, maybe I'd raise a glass, who knows? Luckily, Clay interceded and somehow convinced them to take the party elsewhere. Knowing Clay, he probably gave them an open tab in the lobby bar. My husband could be a killer but he's more the killer-with-kindness type. Dom Pérignon for everyone—except me, of course.

CHAPTER 8

Not Losing Hope Despite a Grim Diagnosis

The next day we flew home to Orlando. In hindsight I should have listened to Clay when he said (multiple times) that I wasn't ready to fly. However, I'm stubborn as all get-out and I'd be damned before admitting I wasn't okay. By the time we got to the airport I was throwing up. The gas pain in my shoulders was unbearable and I kept blacking out. Throw up, black out, repeat—another glimpse of my alternate life as a drug addict. Horrifying. Clay upgraded us to first class and I was unconscious for the entire flight. When we landed, I barely recognized myself as I was wheeled past the glass wall barriers protecting me from the oncoming terminal tram. The following day I went straight back to work. I pushed myself too hard and ended up quite sick. Why must I do this to myself? It becomes glaringly obvious that this is an area that requires work. This obsessive need to be high-functioning and this refusal to allow time to heal.

After a week, I'm mostly healed. I have four small incisions on my lower abdomen but they heal rather quickly. I'm left with three scars that remind me daily to advocate for myself. Eventually, these scars embolden me to advocate for others, but we'll get to that later on.

We waited for two months to receive the test results from the massive blood draw. When the phone rang for my immune panel review, I was waiting in my car with notebook in hand. Dr. Braverman came on the line and I held my breath.

"Hi, Laura," he said, sounding despondent. "Well, this is an extremely difficult case," he expelled.

My hands started shaking and my peripheral vision started to flicker darkness. I could feel my breath start to become short and my pulse begin to quicken. That little voice of mine chimed in: *failure*.

I sat in my car picturing my hero in his Manhattan office surrounded by all of his books with my files scattered all around him. It would be hot in the city now, and I wonder if he's got a window air-conditioning unit. I visualize the red pen marks all over my paperwork and Dr. Braverman rubbing his kind but strained eyes. I wonder if he's lost any sleep over me yet. I wonder how vexing I must be to him, this man that can't sleep until he fixes everything. There I sat, the "extremely difficult" case— the outlier.

"DON'T LOSE HOPE—I WILL GET YOU A BABY."

When I tune back in, he is explaining that it will be impossible for Clay and me to have a biological child without vast medical intervention.

". . . anti-paternal HLA antibodies," he states. My body has developed an allergic reaction to Clay's genetic material.

". . . your body will attack every embryo," he went on. He lists medications and statistics and protocol that we could use, but nothing is guaranteed. "I don't have enough research on cases like yours," he says sadly.

I wondered, possibly out loud, if this meant that I could have pizza again. Not the gluten-free kind, the real deal: thin crust, double gluten for this girl.

"Don't lose hope—I will get you a baby," I hear him say, but I was far away, adrift in a dark sea with no light on the horizon.

After the line went dead, I sat for a while in the parking lot at work. I checked my calendar and cursed my next meeting. The little voice chimed in, *"Cancel the meeting. It's okay to be sad."* But I knew that little voice to be fickle and didn't want to face the guilt later.

I type a text to my assistant. "How do I tell my husband I'm allergic to him?" Delete, delete, delete. "I'll be in soon," I type.

Over the next few days, the reality sets in like the fog that rolled in over the River Tyne when I was a child—thick, relentless, and blinding. I reread my results to the point of memorization and scour the internet for studies until I can't see straight. I have two additional calls with Dr. Braverman to re-review my labs so that I can better understand the meaning and our options. Dr. Braverman is incredibly patient and gracious but begs me to be cautious, as he feels a pregnancy without medication before conception will end in demise. He begs me to be patient as we navigate the insurance approval for treatment and medication.

"Your immune system attacks the embryo. It's the same mechanism that occurs when a patient rejects an organ transplant. Usually the immune system downregulates to accept an embryo, but yours ramps up. Our best shot is a therapy for organ transplant recipients," he explains.

"*Our*," I thought, *how nice*. The therapy, intravenous immunoglobulin, or IVIg, was not approved by my insurance company. The out-of-pocket cost is in the tens of thousands. I fight for months. I fight everyone in my path and even those desperately trying to get off my path. I write, revise, and submit appeal after appeal in an effort to get the therapy approved. For a solid year, I speak with my Cigna representative weekly. I plead, beg, and facilitate meetings between Dr. Braverman and Cigna's medical director. But to no avail. They deny all of the research and all of the hours of appeals. To echo Dr. Braverman: "There's just not enough research," they conclude. "Denied."

But finally, I surrender. Selah.

CHAPTER 9

My Labs Confirm What My Heart Already Knew

I FIRED DOCTORS THAT DIDN'T LIKE IT AND I HIRED DOCTORS THAT SHARED MY PASSION AND PUSHED FOR MY SUCCESS.

This is the part of the story where the book title begins to make sense. While I was fighting for treatment coverage, I was simultaneously building a phenomenal medical team and working on my *self*. The change started the moment I collapsed screaming during my third miscarriage. In that moment I realized what was happening to me was not "normal." Back-to-back, unexplained pregnancy loss is not—nor has it ever been—normal. One miscarriage is common, but as Dr. Braverman said to me on that cold March morning in 2018, "common" doesn't mean "normal." Two miscarriages, three, four—there is absolutely nothing common or normal about it. When I realized this, I shifted from a victim mentality to a mentality of self-advocacy and action. I stopped being passive and started asking questions—lots of them. I started pushing for answers, real ones. I stopped accepting half-ass answers or statistics from outdated and badly managed studies. In short, I stood up for myself. I armed myself with knowledge gained by hours upon hours of research. I stopped being the least educated in the room about my body and started speaking their language. I fired doctors that didn't like it and I hired doctors that shared my passion and pushed for my success. News flash: They do exist.

The transformation, once I truly committed, took eight months. Two hundred and forty days of choosing to be the best version of myself every single day. Don't get me wrong, I had days where I was not the best version of myself. I had moments where I was the absolute worst version of myself. The difference was, over the months, I developed mechanisms by which to cope with the chaos. I rewrote the way I conversed with myself. I rewired my entire mindset. I had a reckoning with God. Allow me to explain every step that brought me to where I am now: a place of Grace.

In April of 2018, I began working with Aimee Raupp, an acupuncturist specializing in women's health and wellness. It was a month after meeting with Dr. Braverman and having surgery with Dr. Vidali. Dr. Braverman recommended a women's health and wellness expert. He said he suspected I had a gluten intolerance and probably a gene mutation called "MTHFR" which would require me to remove folic acid from my diet and take a methylfolate supplement.

Although I thought he was wrong, I reached out to Aimee and set up a consult. She offered free consults so I felt like I hit the lottery twice in a row. The moment I spoke with Aimee on the phone, I felt at ease. Based on my history, she agreed with Dr. Braverman and asked me to trust her. *Trust . . . hmmm, that's a tough one, Aimee.* This was new to me and I wasn't sure if I could do it. After all, every single doctor I had ever worked with had betrayed my trust and completely let me down. But I ordered her book, *Body Belief*, and decided to keep an open mind. The first chapter of the book had a "red flag" symptom list. I stared at it and mentally marked a few items that pertained to me then continued reading. Halfway into the next chapter, I stopped and went back to the list. *You're only lying to yourself,* the little voice chimed in. I took out a pen and went through the list again. After I read each item, I paused and considered. Much to my horror, I checked off forty-two of the symptoms of autoimmune disorder. *What the hell, forty-two? How could this be?* I had been seeing doctors every couple of months for seven years. I could not possibly have this many issues and not a single one of them had flagged them. *How could I not have flagged them?* Houston, we have a problem. An extensive list of problems.

The red flags were indicators of inflammation and potentially autoimmune disease. Three or more symptoms reoccurring on a regular basis was the parameter given. Much of the list was "normal" for me. Things like anxiety, brain fog, mood swings, eczema, and irritability. Some of the things were less prevalent, such as itchy ears, swelling of the ankles, dark circles under the eyes, floaters in vision. And then there was the big one: fertility challenges and/or miscarriage.

The list shocked me into action. I devoured the rest of the book and implemented all of Aimee's suggestions immediately. The suggestions encompass the whole being and include things like: meditation, diet, mindset, belief systems, coping mechanisms, and even things like beauty products and household cleaners.

The diet recommended to reduce inflammation was very strict. Following the guidelines, I had to stop eating grains, soy, legumes, nightshade vegetables, nuts, dairy, refined sugars, and high-glucose fruits.

The first two weeks were absolute hell. I was dizzy, irritable, starving, and had a constant headache. There were days that I'd cry into the refrigerator because I didn't know what to eat and I was so angry that I couldn't eat whatever I wanted. I would see pregnant women all over town sipping on sodas and chowing down on burgers. Social media was littered with mamas-to-be enjoying coffee or a slice of pizza. I was so incredibly angry.

> *You are the culmination of all of your ancestors. You are worthy of healing. You are not your grief. It's okay to be happy.*

But then the fog lifted. The withdrawals came to an end. I was addicted to sugar, gluten, dairy, and carbs. I learned about the benefits of eating like our ancestors did. I introduced bone broth and liver. We completely revamped my supplement game and introduced collagen and gelatin into my daily routine. About six weeks in, I felt incredible. I felt lighter, more energetic, clear minded, and grounded. My grief, anxiety, and depression began to subside. I began to feel alive again for the first time in six years. Hello, old friend.

The forty-two red flags? Well, that was just the beginning. The real work far surpasses the physical self. I began doing weekly guided meditations. In the beginning, it felt very uncomfortable and strained. I was constantly having to redirect my attention and my breathing. The meditations were often a source of additional frustration for me because I just couldn't get out of my own head. *Did I turn the stove off? Did I pack Jolene's snack? What should I make for dinner?* And then some much more sinister thoughts would inevitably creep in: *You can't do this. You're not capable of carrying a pregnancy to term. Why can't you focus? You're wasting your time.* But I showed up every week and eventually, every day. I replayed the meditations over and over until I finally started to feel myself slowing down. It wasn't like all of a sudden I was great at meditating; shoot, I still get distracted. But slowly, the words began to resonate and my self-talk started to shift. It sounded more like this: *Of course you turned the stove off. You never forget Jolene's snack. You have dinner ready because you made enough for two meals.* Then the more sinister thoughts looked like these: *Maybe you can do this. You are capable of carrying a pregnancy—look at Jolene! Your focus is improving. This is helping.*

A TYPICAL DAY WHEN I WAS AT MY MOST COMMITTED

- Within fifteen minutes of waking up, I'd drink hot water with lemon and collagen.
- While drinking my water, I'd slowly begin opening the blinds and turning on the lights in the house. I was silent as I sipped.
- In my head, I'd start repeating affirmations: *You are the culmination of all your ancestors. You are worthy of healing. You are not your grief. It's okay to be happy.*
- I'd have breakfast about an hour later. It was always protein, fat, and greens. Cooked, warm food. I'd take my morning supplements with breakfast and swallow them with the intention of wellness. For the rest of the day, I'd aim to eat every two to three hours. Small meals, always protein, healthy fats, and greens. I'd snack on things like bone broth with sauteed spinach, avocado, and egg yolk, or sweet potato with ghee. Lunch and dinner were meals like salmon with roe, brussels sprouts, and turnip or steak with broccoli, beets, and lots of ghee. Throughout the day I'd drink tons of water and coconut milk.
- I ended each day with a magnesium salt bath.
- I'd spend time reflecting on the day and visualizing the future.
- I'd pray.

I began working with a BodyTalk practitioner, Carolyn Johnson. She lives in Hawaii and would call me monthly for our appointments. We'd talk about my fears and she'd help me breathe through all of the trauma that came bubbling up to the surface. I'd listen as she assured me over and over that I was supported and loved. Slowly, I began to believe her.

I started opening up to people about what I was struggling with. I found myself opening up to complete strangers and receiving genuinely helpful advice. One such stranger suggested I start getting acupuncture with his good friend, Saima Bhatti. I balked. *Needles?! How in the heck will that help me quell anxiety?* The thought alone makes my heart skip a beat. But I made an appointment with another, highly recommended fertility acupuncturist. She had a baby "wall of fame" in her waiting room. At my first appointment, I stared at the pictures and held my breath. I examined the tiny toes and smooshed noses silently. As I was escorted into the treatment room, I felt timid and wondered how this could be helpful.

I had several sessions with this practitioner and every time I left feeling heavily sedated and exhausted. She worked mostly on my back pain and seemed a bit overwhelmed by my extensive reproductive history. I purchased a package with the clinic, but before I made it halfway through the sessions, I stopped seeing her. I was discouraged and unsure if it was the practitioner or the art. I wasn't sure how to proceed or if I should pursue additional support in this arena.

A month or so later, while attending a work function, I struck up a conversation with a massage therapist. We spoke for an hour about wellness, women, and fertility. I left with her card and sat on it for months. Melissa Sonnenschein Cucci. And then I ran into the person that initially recommended acupuncture again. He asked if I had ever seen Saima and I nervously admitted that I hadn't but did intend to. When I finally pulled up her website, I was awestruck to read that she shared her practice with Melissa, the warm wellness-warrior I had met several months prior. Things seemed to be falling into place with ease. It was as if the universe was saying, "You're on the right track."

Saima was an instant ally. She could feel my trepidation and helped me work through it.

"You're incredible," she said, in awe, after we discussed my health plan and goals.

"Ummm, thank you," I stammered.

"You can do this," she said as she held my hand. To my surprise, I didn't feel the urge to pull back.

> *"I'm scared," I replied. "But I believe you."*

"I'm scared," I replied. "But I believe you."

I began seeing Saima as often as she recommended. I'd drive 45 minutes across town once a week, but it never felt like a chore. Acupuncture was scary for me in the beginning. I found it hard to surrender and relax. However, over time, I'd find myself drifting to sleep halfway through each session. I'd wake up smiling as Saima would quietly reenter the room to check my pulse. "How are you feeling?" she'd whisper.

"Relaxed," I'd murmur back.

Our sessions weren't often because by the time I began working with her, my body was very balanced and my mind was mostly calm. As a result, the moment something was "off," I knew it was time for acupuncture. As we progressed with treatment, Saima began encouraging me to surrender even further and one day, I agreed. Once the needles were placed, I began to drift. I began chanting silently to myself, *Please come, please stay.* And sure enough, she came. I felt her immediately, completely overpowering and entirely possessive. I began spinning and felt almost as if I were drowning. It was as if she was saying: "Prepare for me, I am very strong." Overwhelmed, I shouted out for Saima and she came into the room immediately. She worked for ten minutes to reground and center me.

"You are strong too," she said, without a word spoken by me. Frequently, when people tell me I am strong, I feel conflicted. I have had four miscarriages. When I say that aloud, I often don't feel anything; I feel disconnected. People often ask stupid and insensitive questions about my miscarriages and I do feel the sting of those, so I'm definitely still alive. Sometimes I feel embarrassed and ashamed, weak and like a failure. My body is rebelling against my heart and my mind, and it has been for years now as I've tried to "be strong."

> *I had finally given up the power struggle and no longer needed to be the strongest person in the room.*

The world seems to idolize strong people, but my strength is a double-edged sword. I have built all of my relationships, my entire world, on the premise of this "strength." I am dominant, I am stubborn, I am determined, and I am cold. I power through. Just like I was taught. Because the moment I'm weak, I have to hear everything I've been tuning out for years. What do you do when you can't be strong anymore? The experience I had during my acupuncture session shook me to my core on a physical, emotional, and spiritual level. Several days later I invited the lovely spirit who asked me to prepare for her back, and again she drowned me. I sat up gasping and felt so incredibly small. Two weeks later, I tried again. This time I didn't move against her. I simply let go and allowed myself to spin. The surrender was becoming a habit. After about twenty minutes, the spinning lessened and as I slowly opened my eyes I knew that I was truly ready. I had finally given up the power struggle and no longer needed to be the strongest person in the room.

Sure enough, my labs confirmed what my heart already knew. I was ready to try and conceive again. My vitamin D level was in the optimal range for fertility, all of my thyroid numbers looked perfect, my fatty acids were at an excellent ratio, and my inflammation was almost nonexistent. I was finished preparing for my sixth pregnancy. Dr. Braverman, Dr. Vidali, Aimee Raupp, Carolyn Johnson, and Saima Bhatti all gave me the green light to proceed. We decide to try to get pregnant via intrauterine insemination (IUI) rather than the "natural" route. There are a lot of moving parts, especially managing the medications, so IUI offers a better level of control over the variables.

CHAPTER 10

Please Come, Please Stay

It's April 2019 and Dr. Braverman has passed away unexpectedly. The shock is palpable and I am devastated. Most people can't comprehend the loss of a hero because most people idolize someone they don't really know. This man was known to me. This man went to bat for me. This man was my hope.

As I read the news, tears stream down my cheeks. I shout to Clay, who's in the shower, "Dr. Braverman has died!" After he dries off, we sit in disbelief repeating over and over, "I can't believe it." A couple of hours later I begin to come out of my stupor and through sniffs I speak, "I don't trust anyone else."

I get up early the next day. My eyes are puffy from crying and I feel foggy. I slip quietly from our bedroom and make my way downstairs in the dark. I sit and sip lemon ginger tea and picture Dr. Braverman responding to my emails from what must have been his deathbed. The tears flow freely now with nobody watching. I look to the sky, still dusky, and pray. I ask Dr. B to continue to fight for me. I ask him to usher my baby from the heavens. I ask him to forgive himself and say, "You'll finally get some sleep, warrior." I walk back inside and make both breakfast and lunch. As I finish my tea, I hear Jolene beginning to stir. I wipe my face and announce, "Breakfast is ready!"

I spend the day networking. I find it hard to smile as people congratulate me on a recent award. I say, "Thank you, I'm excited," and wonder if they can see my sadness. If they can, they don't let on, and the day proceeds as if nothing happened. As if my life hadn't shifted dramatically, again. By 7:00 p.m., I've deteriorated into panic. "Who will manage my care?" I wonder out loud. We have a pending IUI in three weeks and the terror is setting in. "How do I do this without him?"

It becomes glaringly obvious that my confidence was deeply rooted in the ability of my medical team; the team that took me half a decade to find and build. With my leader gone, I have two choices: find a new leader or lead myself. My heart tells me, loudly, to stay the course. You are ready.

Saturday, June 8th, 2019.
Day one of my cycle. I started spotting yesterday evening but it was too late to get in for an ultrasound—the office was closed for the weekend. Looks like I'll have to wait until Monday for my baseline scan. I set my alarm for 7:00 a.m. and call as soon as the office opens on Monday morning. Let's do this. When they don't pick up after four attempts, I begin to worry.

Because it's now day three of my cycle, I need to begin my IUI protocol. Do I risk this without checking my uterine lining and follicle count? If I have a cyst, would the letrozole that stimulates ovulation make it worse and jeopardize this month altogether? By 2:00 p.m., it's pouring and I decide to make the forty-five-minute drive to Maitland. The rain makes the commute at least an hour, and when I pull up to dark windows and an empty parking lot my heart sinks. Did they close? Have they been arrested? Did my reproductive endocrinologist die too? I am spiraling.

When I get home, I decide to begin the medication. I've already begun my autoimmune medications and figure not starting the letrozole would essentially be throwing in the towel. I choose hope over fear and pray that the office is open in the morning. Choosing hope over fear is something I have to be intentional about. In order for mindfulness to become habit, we must practice.

Tuesday, June 11th, 2019.
I'm up at 4:00 a.m. My anxiety is heightened by the medications and I'm starving. When the office doesn't pick up the phone at opening time, I'm on the road by 7:15. When I pull up there's one car in the lot, and I'm elated! I push through the door to find the IVF coordinator standing in the reception area. "Are you open?" I stammer. Her expression tells me something is off and she doesn't know who I am. "I'm a patient!" I explain. And with that, she proceeds to tell me that a thunderstorm has taken their phones and internet offline. Thankfully, the ultrasound machine is working and she agrees to check me on the spot.

"Wow, your lining is gorgeous!" she exclaims. "I see no reason we can't proceed with IUI this month!" Game on.

The following morning, Day 5, I'm back in Maitland for my first intralipid infusion. Intralipids are essential fatty acids that they put straight into the bloodstream. I'm not sure what to expect but it's relatively quick and painless. I had a mild headache for a couple of days but otherwise felt normal.

Monday, June 17th, 2019: Day 10 of my cycle.
The ultrasound looks good and my reproductive endocrinologist, or RE, tells me I'm really close. He needs me to return the following morning to confirm and says excitedly, "I'm thinking the first IUI will be Wednesday!" The following day my follicle count and maturity look great and my lining is the praise of the office. We schedule the double IUI for Wednesday and Thursday mornings at 8:00 a.m. A hormonal injection, referred to as a trigger shot, is to be given at 8:00 p.m. the evening before.

Wednesday, June 19th, 2019: Day 12 of my cycle.
I'm so anxious as Clay and I walk into the clinic. Clay bought me roses to, as he said, "keep things kinda romantic." He carries them into the office along with macaroons for the entire staff. "If you get nervous just smell this rose," he smiles.

I lie there in the dark room listening to the hum of the ultrasound machine. I glance occasionally at the grainy screen and try not to picture the images that haunt me in my weaker moments. I close my eyes and whisper to myself, *You'll never have a bad ultrasound again.* When the doctor comes in, I've worked myself into a slightly tense state of anxiety. He's very calming and reminds me to relax. "You're a super responder!" he says, looking at the image of my ovaries on the screen. "I can't believe how great this looks. You're ready!" Deep breaths. Dr. McNichol understands the power of words.

On Thursday, I'm back for the second IUI but this time I'm alone. Clay had to fly to Houston for a meeting. I wish I'd remembered to bring a rose. I'm very used to doing things alone, but getting pregnant isn't one of them. After the procedure I'm able to completely relax and visualize everything going perfectly. I feel very at peace and hopeful. As I leave the office, I schedule blood work to check my progesterone along with my heparin levels. When I get home that evening, I begin my twice-daily injections of Lovenox, a blood thinner that works to make the blood flow without coagulation between mother and baby through the placenta, and up my immune dosages, which will help my body tolerate the pregnancy.

My progesterone level comes back low and we immediately begin supplementation. I worry that I have somehow manifested this, as I had been concerned my progesterone would be an issue. During my last pregnancy, I was on progesterone injections and felt deeply traumatized by them—something in the recesses of my mind was still clinging to this. My support group assures me that the levels will rise and we caught it quickly enough. All I can do is pray.

Tuesday, July 2nd, 2019: Day 25 of my cycle.
I've now officially taken twenty-one at-home pregnancy tests. With the exception of a couple of extremely faint "shadow lines," all of them have been negative. I know it's early and I'm trying

not to lose hope, but it's hard and I feel despondent. The early signs of pregnancy very much resemble the onset of a menstrual cycle—a cruel coincidence. I'm feeling some mild lower back cramping and some tightening sensations in my uterus, but neither of these are conclusive evidence of anything. Occasionally, my breasts feel sensitive, and I think, *What have we here?!* but the thought is fleeting, and the thrill gives way to doubt.

Friday, July 5th, 2019: Beta Day.
My appointment is at 8:15 a.m. so I'm out the door by 6:45 so my dad can give me my Lovenox injection before I drive across town. Jolene is tired and resistant to my attempts at waking her gently. She's grumpy and asks if she can stay in her pajamas. I don't argue and strap her into her car seat then hand her breakfast to-go. I've lost most hope at this point but need to be sure.

I'VE NOW OFFICIALLY TAKEN TWENTY-ONE AT-HOME PREGNANCY TESTS.

I pull into the office and sit for a second before turning off my car. I whisper desperately, *Please come, please stay.* The nurse, Yani, greets me and says it's possible that we'll have a different result in the blood work. She assures me that they'll let me know by lunchtime. By 2:00 p.m., I'm impatient. I call the office at 2:30. Yani has left for the day but the doctor will call me shortly. I feel as though I've been punched in the gut. *This doesn't bode well,* I think to myself. An hour later, still no call and I can't resist calling back. Dr. McNichol gets on the line and confirms what I've known in my heart for a couple of days: the beta was negative. I hang up the phone and draw myself a bath. As I slide in, I whisper, *Please come, please stay.*

I have to immediately cease the Lovenox and Zarxio, along with cutting my Plaquenil dose in half. When I wake up the next morning, I feel as though I've been hit by a bulldozer. I'm shocked at the intensity of the withdrawals and wonder how I'm going to drag myself out of bed. The next couple of days are a blur as my body and heart adjust. I'm sad but not devastated, tired but not exhausted. When my cycle starts the following Tuesday, I'm excited and feel ready to begin again. This time I won't take multiple pregnancy tests each day but instead I'll breathe and be patient. I'll trust more and try to control less. Selah.

> *This time I won't take multiple pregnancy tests each day but instead I'll breathe and be patient. I'll trust more and try to control less. Selah.*

Saturday, August 3rd, 2019.
I'm pregnant. We're twelve days post IUI and I've got a positive pink line on my tiny hCG home test strip. It's 1:30 a.m. and I'm alone. It's completely silent in the house but my heart is screaming. *Hello number six!* I manage to get ahold of Clay. He's on night shift so he's awake and speechless. By 2:00 a.m., I've emailed my immunologist and endocrinologist: "Positive Beta," the subject line reads. "We need to schedule an immune panel ASAP," the body reads. No room for pleasantries; my body could already be reacting, attacking, killing.

When I wake the next morning I take another test—still positive. I assess my symptoms: no nausea . . . yet. Just a slight sense of fogginess and fatigue. My parents are still sleeping when I pull up for my morning Lovenox injection. As they rise sleepily, I explain we can't be lenient with the timing because things are a lot more serious now. They look at me inquisitively and it clicks. They're cautiously optimistic and my dad washes his hands in preparation.

On Monday I wake up to spotting. The coloring is very dull so I'm almost positive it's implantation bleeding. Still, never a nice sight, and my throat starts to tighten with anxiety. Nevertheless, the first beta comes back positive at a level of twenty-five. I allow myself to feel excited and download the pregnancy tracker, "What to Expect When You're Expecting." As I log into the account I created eight years ago, I wonder if I'm doing the right thing. I've had to delete three pregnancies from this platform and the most recent one, our fourth miscarriage, is still lingering in here. I take a deep breath, hit "delete pregnancy," and enter the new pregnancy. It's over in several seconds and somehow feels therapeutic. The due date is generated, the gestational age pops up, and I feel warm. Two days later, my beta has more than doubled to a level of seventy-four and my progesterone is at twenty-nine. So far, this looks promising! My immune panel is a whopping eighteen vials followed by an intralipid IV infusion. My dad drives me around town all day because I'm too lightheaded to drive myself. He takes me to lunch and gets me steak frites with lots of salt and jus. I feel rejuvenated and cared for and hope starts creeping in.

Monday, August 19th, 2019.

In three days I have my first ultrasound. I'll be six weeks and one day and my baby could have a heartbeat. We should be able to see what resembles a tadpole, a small comma of cells and energy nestled into my uterus. Up until this morning, I've been excited. But today the tone shifted, and I had to leave work early after a mild panic attack set in. The thoughts started creeping in shortly before lunch and spiraled quickly out of control. My mind began screaming, *Everyone else is going to get their baby except you!* And it became a loop. Once I got home, I was able to calm myself, but it took a couple of hours. I ran myself a bath, put on my guided meditation, and started reworking my mental conversation. I sat in the darkness visualizing a beautiful image on the ultrasound screen. I pulled out pictures of Jolene's first ultrasound and said out loud, "See! You can do this. You have done this!" After my bath, I made myself egg yolks and sweet potato wedges. I ate slowly and sipped on lemon tea and let myself be scared. Learning to honor my emotions rather than run from them has brought me so much peace.

The ultrasound is perfect. We see and hear a heartbeat and everything looks fine. I've been here before, though, so I struggle to feel the excitement a first-time mom would feel. Or a mom that hasn't experienced miscarriage. I reflect on this with sadness in my heart. I long to shed the fear and worry. I long to celebrate the pregnancy and ultrasound without any nagging voice in the recesses whispering, "Not yet. It's too early."

In the first trimester I have to get blood work every couple of days for various reasons. We track hCG every two days for a week and progesterone every three days. In addition, I have to get large blood draws to monitor my immune system every two weeks. The big draws are a lot. I have to drive to a private lab across town and coordinate with a specialty lab in New Jersey. The box of vials arrives in advance of me with instructions for the phlebotomist. I have to bring dry ice with me so that half of the vials can be shipped back frozen. The other half are not frozen, and I constantly worry that the phlebotomist will mix them up. One of my lab draws falls on what Florida calls a "Hurricane Day," meaning most of the state goes into total panic mode and empties the shelves of grocery stores and home improvement stores. Gas becomes scarce and the mail functionality screeches to a snail's pace. I can't find dry ice anywhere (people stockpile it in case they lose power and need to keep things cold), and I'm in tears as I call every store within a fifty-mile radius. *Why can nothing be easy?* I wonder, full of irritation. This matters immensely, because if my immune system is reacting my immunologist needs to adjust my medication. He would need to do this very quickly in the hopes of dampening the reaction and saving my baby. Somehow, Clay manages to find what is probably the last dry ice in Orlando and we are able to ship out the blood samples. Unfortunately, the mail fails us and I end up having to redraw all eleven vials two days later. Thankfully the report comes back fine and we don't need to adjust the meds, but I can't tell you the amount of anxiety that consumed those days. It's hard when you can't yet feel the baby kicking to confirm everything is on track. I lived for and dreaded the days that included an ultrasound.

  I have to get three intralipid infusions. Each infusion takes a couple of hours and, as with all of my appointments, is across town. With each draw I get less anxious about the needles. With each day I do better with the injections. My lower abdomen quickly becomes a deep purple bruise from the twice-daily Lovenox. We move over to my hips and then my love handles. Within a few weeks I've run out of skin to inject that isn't bruised and we have to move to the thighs while the rest of my skin heals. As my belly continues to stretch it becomes harder to pinch the skin, so we start injecting directly into my skin without trying to pinch it and this seems to bruise less. The blood draws consistently come back without cause for concern. My immune system is tolerating the pregnancy and my hormones are adjusting appropriately. For the first time in my life, I'm pregnant without hyperemesis gravidarum. My blood sugar is stable and the prednisone also helps quell nausea. I think back on everything I did to support my body and prepare for this pregnancy and I'm so proud. Hyperemesis isn't something one can explain—it's hard to imagine a temporary sickness could be so incredibly debilitating, but I'm not exaggerating when I say that I questioned trying to conceive again based on the possibility of hyperemesis.

> *Learning to honor my emotions rather than run from them has brought me so much peace.*

The first trimester continues in this fashion: On a slow week I have three appointments. Usually, I have five. In addition to the typical fatigue that accompanies the first trimester, the endless appointments are exhausting. I will say, though, each appointment reassures me and quells the anxiety. A big part of medical self-advocacy is pushing for extra support. Extra support in the form of appointments, answers, lab work, and referrals. The amount of support I experience is incredible. My reproductive immunologist, reproductive endocrinologist, and acupuncturist check on me constantly. The labs are responsive and respectful. Everyone is gracious, kind, and patient with me. I ask millions of questions, request additional lab work and ultrasounds. My numbers, results, and ultrasounds continue to be excellent.

At the recommendation of my endocrinologist, Dr. McNichol, I get genetic testing done at the nine-week mark. The paperwork includes the option to check the gender. I check "yes" although I'm thoroughly convinced the baby is a girl. The testing is done through blood work, so I submit to another "it-will-feel-like-a-bee-sting" prick. Thankfully, the results come back quickly and the baby is at low risk for genetic abnormalities. The nurse asks if I'd like to know the gender and I'm grinning from ear to ear. It's a girl. Isla. Everything starts to feel more real. Perhaps even tangible.

At twelve weeks I begin seeing my ob-gyn, Dr. Bartfield, in addition to my reproductive endocrinologist. My RE isn't quite ready to let me go fully and continues to monitor me until fourteen weeks. When I walk into my ob-gyn's office, I'm very nervous. I'm fearful that they won't be as supportive as my RE or as proactive about testing and monitoring. I already know they will be supportive of the protocol from my reproductive immunologist so that, at least, is a relief. Dr. Bartfield walks in and smiles. He sits down and takes a deep breath. He's holding my chart and when he looks at me, I can see that he is emotional. He proceeds with our appointment and explains that he will do everything in his power to support me and help me get to term. He can't believe everything I've been through and suggests we add a maternal-fetal medicine specialist to my care team. Several of my close friends have been under the care of an MFM, so I'm familiar with what they do. I gladly accept the recommendation, and he refers me to Dr. Armando Fuentes.

Luckily, Dr. Fuentes practices at a large hospital in my neighborhood. This means I can schedule the appointments very early in the morning before work. It also means he's very close if I need something urgently. It's not the first time I've visited this hospital. When Jolene was a baby, we had to take her to their emergency room after she tripped and bashed her tooth on her toddler bed frame. There was blood everywhere and I thought she was definitely going to lose the tooth. The accident also happened to occur on the day of my bridal shower, so the last time I was here I was pretty fancy, covered in blood, and escorting a hysterical little girl. As I walked into the lobby, I hoped this experience would be much calmer. Because I'm an overly punctual person, I arrived before the maternal-fetal clinic opened. But the door was open, so I quietly entered their waiting area and sat myself down in a chair facing the receptionist desk. The lights were dim and for a moment I considered leaving

> *They treat this pregnancy as one unto its own. It's an incredibly refreshing approach. They are obviously aware of my traumatic past; however, they focus entirely on this pregnancy. This baby. My sixth baby.*

as quietly as I'd entered. Such a detailed ultrasound would be daunting in most pregnancies because they're literally looking for problems. As I willed myself to stay seated, the receptionist arrived and brought me crashing back down to earth.

"Name, please?" she queried.

"Laura Fletcher," I mumbled as the acid in my stomach began to rise and little black dots began to crowd my peripheral vision. Deep breaths. Stand up slowly.

The appointment goes very well. The team members are kind and thorough and very considerate of my circumstances. They don't ask questions about things that are clearly spelled out in my chart. They treat this pregnancy as one unto its own. It's an incredibly refreshing approach. They are obviously aware of my traumatic past; however, they focus entirely on *this* pregnancy. *This* baby. My sixth baby. I sit up, clean myself off, and get dressed. I make my next appointment on my way out and slip quietly out of the waiting room back into the lobby of the hospital. The room is brilliant with sunshine and I whisper out loud to myself: "Selah."

I walk through the sunshine to the parking garage, where I carefully climb into my car. I clip my seat belt in and adjust the waist belt to sit under my barely showing bump. I sit for a moment working up the courage to drive back out into the world where I will begin the countdown until my next ultrasound. Pregnancy after loss is living from one appointment to the next. As I slide the gear into drive, I call my mom and tell her everything looks fine. She is elated.

During my previous pregnancies it was almost impossible to work during the first trimester. I was sick so often that I spent most of my day running to the bathroom and then dragging myself up off the cold, pink marble floor. I was working in sales for Norman's at The Ritz-Carlton for my first five pregnancies and the very beginning of my sixth. Norman's was a fine dining restaurant where everything was made from scratch. I had to avoid the kitchen at all costs because the smell of simmering broth and garlic was

> *"You will never have a bad ultrasound again."*

lethal to me. When the restaurant closed down, I found myself wanting to say goodbye to the areas I had spent years of my life in. This, undoubtedly, included the lavish bathroom that saw the worst of my hyperemesis. In a way it was cathartic to walk out for the last time, as if I were putting the hyperemesis behind me.

This pregnancy is different, I remind myself as I drive the forty-five minutes to my new office. "You will never have a bad ultrasound again," I say out loud over and over and over. It is an anthem, a plea to God, and a war cry all rolled into one. If I say it often enough, loud enough, with enough conviction, maybe it will become my reality.

Two of my closest fertility friends are pregnant. "Fertility friends" are what I call the fierce and fast friendships formed with women all over the world struggling with the same challenges as me. These friendships are different. They don't have boundaries. They don't actually feel like a separate person having a separate experience. They feel like the collective "I." The understanding and support is so deep and so thorough that we almost merge. We have gotten to a place where we feel each other's emotional states even though we are continents away. They are terrified and elated at the same time about their pregnancies. They simultaneously want to celebrate and hide away. Stuff down their emotions and also shout from the rooftops, "I'm PREGNANT!!" But they don't. They whisper to each other, to me, to their partners: "I'm pregnant." They hold their breath as they wait for the reaction. Will our loved ones cower or rise up? Will they exclaim or clench their jaws? Will they rattle off assurance or withhold hope? The cycle of testing begins for them. The beta tests, the progesterone tests, the at-home pee-on-a-stick-and-then-hold-your-breath tests, and the immune tests. The big panels that make us feel woozy and see black spots in our peripheral vision. We lose sleep. We hold each other from afar and pray, and pray, and pray. I share with them my war cry: "You will never have a bad ultrasound again." They adopt the anthem. They repeat it to themselves daily and even more so on appointment days. They see their betas rise appropriately and their progesterone flourish. They see the yolk sac, the fetal pole, and the heartbeat. We all live in joy and terror every moment of the nine months we're pregnant.

    I cannot express to you the vital importance of these bonds, these friendships. Here's what I know: Nobody in your life will understand your anguish unless they too have experienced your pain. I often found the people I was closest to were the ones that blundered the most in supporting me through a miscarriage; not because they had malicious intent—they just couldn't begin to grasp the depth of suffering. Get yourself some women that have walked in your shoes. Link arms with them. Love each other oh-so hard. Their stories are not mine to tell (although I deeply hope they will share them in the near future), but I do want to share a little glimpse into their personalities and the ways in which we supported each other.

FRIENDS IN THE TRENCHES WITH YOU: ALEKSANDRA AND CORTNEY

Aleksandra, my friend in Australia, has fluffy rainbow socks. She wears them to her appointments. She travels long distances to the appointments and has to take a number of transport methods to get where she needs to be. She often messages me en route and shares her incredibly beautiful and insightful thoughts. She and I look for signs from the universe, tokens of hope. Rainbows, bunnies, and energy shifts are always good omens. We tell each other about all of the possible good omens we come across and vehemently agree with each other that they are, indeed, good.

We both follow very specific meal plans. Due to our hyperreactive immune systems, we have to closely monitor and manage our inflammation. We do this through many modalities, but food is a huge factor. We find ways to celebrate our nutrition. Most people complain and feel restricted, but not Aleks. She finds a way to bring grace to every situation. Even the really, really hard ones. It's inspiring. She's inspiring. Sometimes, even now, I hear her soft encouragement when I'm still and centered. When I'm anxious, I find myself looking at my hands and reminding myself that she's always holding onto me even though it would take over twenty-four hours for me to actually stand next to her. When I'm lost for words, I know she'll have just the right ones. She'll know exactly what I need to hear in a way that's so . . . easy. So clear. It's not advice that she shares, it's understanding. She empathizes so beautifully.

continued

I learn so many things from her about compassion and love. She helps me find hope again.

    Aleks sends me pictures of her fluffy feet propped up on the ob-gyn chair. She's waiting for an ultrasound. We're in totally different time zones but I wait up. I wait for her message letting me know everything is okay. I pray and repeat our anthem out loud. I clench my jaw. I release my jaw. I remind myself that Aleks is doing EVERYTHING right. She always lets me know. Because she knows I'm waiting. She knows I'm invested. She knows I'm praying the same prayers she's pleading with the Lord to hear. She never has a bad ultrasound again. Her little one graced us shortly after Isla was born. He came barreling into the world and the energy shifted. A good omen.

∽

Cortney lives in Texas and her personality is as big as the state itself. She's a newborn services specialist and spends most waking hours (and non-waking hours) helping women get the support they need when they're bringing a baby into the world. She's been a mom to so many children over so many years. I often wonder how she does this type of work while she privately longs for her own baby. She's selfless, though. She serves and serves and serves. She nurtures and educates everyone lucky enough to cross paths with her. But there's something she does not do: She does not bullshit. She gives it to you straight every single time. She tells the truth and backs it up with peer-reviewed research in the sweetest voice you ever did hear.

Cortney and I are under the care of the same reproductive immunologist, Dr. Andrea Vidali. In addition to a host of other immune issues, we both have endometriosis. Mine silent; hers, not so much. We both have surgery around the same time in Hoboken, New Jersey. True to our type A personalities, Cortney and I both cut our recovery time short and rush back to work. We're learning to let go but we haven't quite mastered it yet.

For the next few months, we heal. We focus on emotional shifts and we try to forgive ourselves. We start to feel ready, and we begin planning.

Under the careful watch of Dr. Vidali, we're on a multitude of medications. It's so calming to have someone with whom I can discuss dosage, side effects, fears, but mostly: hope. When I get pregnant, Cort gives me tips for injecting Lovenox, a blood thinner, into my bruised and stretched skin. We sound off about the fact that managing fertility treatments is a full-time job and grieve the experience of a "normal" pregnancy. We can say to each other, without fear of backlash or judgment, that it's not fair that we have to jump through so many hoops to do what so many other women sail through with ease. For me, fertility challenges after having a living child have often made me feel like I don't have the right to complain.

Cortney always has so much to give. Her strength was, and is, such a force. She gave birth to her miracle child with her doula by her side. She, like many other women, was

continued

cut off from support due to COVID-19 and had to recover from a C-section with a newborn completely alone. I still weep at not being able to be with her in those moments. Sawyer, up against every odd, arrived—and again, the energy shifted.

No pregnancy after loss feels safe. There are milestones you reach that allow you to breathe a little easier; moments in which you think "Okay, we've got this." But those moments don't last. It's not realistic to expect a worry-free pregnancy after miscarriage. It's especially unrealistic to expect this after recurrent miscarriage. But I promise you, having someone in the trenches next to you helps.

CHAPTER 11

Finally– Another Birth Announcement

It's September. When I hit the second trimester, I'm in disbelief. I've been pregnant six times, but I've only made it to the second trimester twice. We run my final immune panel and everything looks "perfect." Dr. Vidali is the only person I trust to use this word. He is absolutely thrilled with all my immune markers and tells me that I can stop taking the Zarxio and progesterone and start to wean off the prednisone. I start to panic. I'm not sure I can do what he's asking me to do. *What if I stop the meds and Isla dies?* So I ask him. He reassures me that this is a very common reaction and tells me we'll take it slow and watch for any kind of reaction. I'm so scared that I burst into tears.

"Your body is handling this pregnancy beautifully," he says. Dr. Vidali understands the power of words.

That night, I follow his direction. Prednisone is a very strong steroid so even at this early stage of reducing it, I wake up aching the following morning. With the withdrawal symptoms that acute, we decide to take it even slower. I decrease my dose by five milligrams each week. Down from forty milligrams to zero. One of the main side effects of coming off the prednisone is hair loss. I also experienced nausea, fatigue, and mood swings. While taking prednisone, my face was round like a moon. Thankfully, the moon effect lessened as the dosage decreased.

During this time I carried a fetal Doppler in my purse. I used it to detect Isla's heartbeat every time I'd feel anxious and needed reassurance. At work I'd run to the bathroom to quickly check. Sometimes I'd even check at a red light. I woke countless times at night to make sure she was okay. I never listened for long—just long enough to know she was okay. It made a huge difference in my ability to relax and sleep. The Doppler is a tool I recommend to any woman experiencing pregnancy after miscarriage. Or even any expecting mother experiencing heightened anxiety.

At this point, I had to begin reintroducing foods that I'd avoided completely while trying to conceive and during the first trimester. The theory being that Isla would be less likely to have aversions or allergies if exposed in utero. This, too, was very scary for me. For so long I had worked to keep my inflammation low and my immune system neutral. This felt like waving a red flag at a bull. I leaned on Aimee Raupp heavily. We reintroduced things very slowly. Mentally, I had to constantly remind myself that my body was healed and my gut was no longer leaking toxins into my bloodstream, creating a huge inflammatory response. I had spent two years healing, repairing. One step at a time I was able to successfully reintroduce everything with the exception of soy and red pepper.

THE DOPPLER IS A TOOL I RECOMMEND TO ANY WOMAN EXPERIENCING PREGNANCY AFTER MISCARRIAGE. OR EVEN ANY EXPECTING MOTHER EXPERIENCING HEIGHTENED ANXIETY.

It's November 29th, 2019. Twenty weeks into the pregnancy, I'm feeling much surer of it. I decide I'm ready to share the news with my extended family and friends. We announce the pregnancy on social media and I also share that we have had to fight for this child for seven years and have experienced loss and unimaginable heartbreak. The outpouring of support is overwhelming. I can't tell you how many people reached out to me to share that they too have experienced infertility and/or miscarriage. "I had a miscarriage," the messages often read. They ask a lot of questions: What did you do differently? Which prenatal did you take? When did you start seeing a fertility specialist? What did you eat? Did you try acupuncture? These women are encouraged by my story. I feel emboldened by this. Perhaps I can help them the same way Karen helped me. I could usher them in the right direction.

As my pregnancy continues, I keep on sharing. I talk to women at networking events and on social media. On Facebook there are hundreds of forums on miscarriage, pregnancy after miscarriage, infertility, and secondary infertility groups. Women post thousands of questions per day. I start responding. I chime in and provide support. I start connecting with women all over the world. I receive messages from India,

England, Scotland, Canada, and most of the United States. I do my best to help them. I spend hundreds of hours communicating with these women. I learn their stories and they ask about mine. We create a safe space online to share. They ask for advice on everything imaginable, from "What kind of makeup do you recommend?" to "Why do you think I keep miscarrying?" I learn about their whole lives, their hopes, their dreams, and their biggest fears. I start to realize that this is what I'm passionate about. This in itself is part of the healing and part of the bigger picture. Over time I start to find the grace in grief. I become deeply connected to myself. I know myself. I accept myself. I have the opportunity to support and care for other women. I begin to let myself visualize a different career path. One in which a decade of struggle turned to understanding can serve a purpose much bigger than myself.

SCOTLAND

I've wanted a home in Scotland since we moved to the United States when I was seven. Not anywhere in Scotland, but a specific street in a specific town with a very specific view. We've tried to purchase four houses on said street, always to be outbid or overlooked. Early in my pregnancy, a house became available. I immediately wrote to place an offer. Much to my shock, the offer was accepted, and now we're in the throes of buying a second home halfway across the world while in the early stages of a high-risk pregnancy. I'm determined to stay calm and allow for things to proceed as they will. By October of 2019, we officially own the house and decide we'd like to spend Christmas there. My mom flies over in advance to oversee the renovation and furnishing.

I get permission to fly from all my doctors so we book flights for Christmas and start packing. We happen to be on the same flight as a good friend of Clay's, Marc. He's got a first-class ticket and insists I switch seats with him. At first, I decline but quickly realize he really wants to sit with Clay, so I agree. Being able to crawl into a bed on the overnight flight is a kindness this pregnant mama can't repay. It's bliss. We switch back before landing and I start to feel incredibly nauseous. I've had to take my meds on a mostly empty stomach and I'm frantically digging through my carry-on for something to snack on. All I can find is a Vital Proteins Collagen Bar, which makes me feel slightly better. By the time we're on the ground in London, I'm miserable.

continued

We get stuck in an extremely long line at customs and I begin dry heaving. I dry heave so intensely that I pee my pants while trying to make a mad dash to the bathroom. As if it couldn't get any worse, our connecting flight isn't for five hours. We find a restaurant and I pass out curled up on the booth seat until it's time for our flight to Inverness. I feel immensely better to be almost "home."

At this point in my pregnancy it's time to reintroduce gluten. I have been both terrified and excited for this moment. I remind myself that my body is strong and opt for local venison pie with mashed potatoes and vegetables. I order with gusto and rejoice when I have no reaction. A few days later I have a scone with clotted cream and strawberry jam.

I continue with the twice-daily Lovenox injections. I always carry one on me just in case I get stuck somewhere. The injection is no longer intimidating or anxiety-inducing. It's simply part of my morning and evening routines. The bruising isn't quite as bad, but the skin has become hardened so it's challenging to find a suitable spot to inject. I wonder how long these areas will remain tender.

Jolene is overjoyed with the house. Her bedroom is set up in the loft. She has a view over Loch Broom and a canopy of twinkle lights above her bed. She creates a reading nook in the window bay, and I think to myself, *We could peacefully live here.*

Clay makes himself known to everyone in the village with his strong American accent and "everyone's best friend" attitude. We've been coming here for years but I think he feels more like he belongs now. He takes Jolene fishing and we go on nice walks in the winter air. Because the house is new to us and we plan to do short-term rentals, Clay spends a lot of time doing projects with my dad. I wish there was more time to relax and enjoy. I'm pretty sure Clay wishes the same.

We buy and decorate a Christmas tree. It's in the front room and people passing by can see the twinkling lights and roaring fire. *This is exactly what I wanted*, I think, as I drift into a nap on the couch. Whether we are spending Christmas with family in the States or in Scotland, my dad's mom, his cousin, Ruth, her husband, Philip, and their daughter, Melissa, always carry out a Christmas Eve tradition with Jolene. Melissa helps Jolene make reindeer food, which consists of oats and glitter. They sprinkle it up the path to guide the reindeer in while the rest of us sing Christmas carols. It's so cold we can see our breath. Next year, Melissa and Jolene will help Isla make the reindeer food. It's a thought I dare to picture in my mind.

The flight back to Orlando is easier. It's a daytime flight so I don't get as exhausted. I also make sure to eat something every couple of hours. We get home and I'm booked in for an ultrasound the following day. Because I can feel Isla moving all the time now, I'm not as reliant on the ultrasounds for reassurance; however, it's always nice to have confirmation.

CHAPTER 12

Nearing Delivery Under the Shadow of COVID-19

Clay and I get stuck back into work, and Jolene begrudgingly returns to school. For the next few weeks into January 2020 everything is routine and easy. At thirty-four weeks, that changes. I start having contractions while I'm at work. I get dizzy and short of breath. My heart feels like it's going to explode out of my chest. I call my ob-gyn, but I know the drill so I make the call on my way to the emergency room.

"Head straight to triage," he confirms. "One of us will meet you there."

As I approach Winnie Palmer Hospital, I'm not immune to the fact that my best and worst days have happened here. I feel very anxious as I pull into the valet entrance. They open the door and ask if I need assistance.

"I'm not sure," I mumble. "I might be in labor." I decline the offered wheelchair and approach the registration desk.

"Have you been here before?" the woman behind the desk asks, never looking up from her computer.

"Too many times," I offer up.

In triage, they check my blood pressure, weight, and temperature. The nurse not is concerned at all and I can tell by her posture she's completely unaware of my medical history. Surely four miscarriages should prompt a sense of urgency.

I'm ushered into a room shortly afterward. I'm alone and scared. My heart rate is all over the place and I wish that Clay was here. He's at work in the middle of the Gulf of Mexico. He can't get here so I don't know if I should tell him what's going on.

The nurse comes in and hooks me up to tons of monitors. Isla's heart rate is within normal range. My blood pressure is low but my heart rate seems normal. They start an IV to get me some fluids while they continue to monitor me and baby. The contractions taper off with the fluids. The EKG comes back normal too. I call Clay to let him know where I am and why. He calls his office and they agree to helicopter him off the boat the following day. I feel immense relief knowing he's coming home. Since everything looks normal and the contractions taper off, I'm sent home.

My MFM and ob-gyn decide we should begin weekly biophysical stress test ultrasounds. During a biophysical, specific markers for distress, such as movement, heart rate, and practice breaths, are tracked. Isla passes each exam, but the ultrasounds also show that she's breech. Her head is nuzzled into my right rib cage. This explains why I've had to see a chiropractor for misplaced ribs for the last few weeks. Dr. Bartfield suggests a handful of at-home methods to encourage proper positioning and tells me that we still have plenty of time. But when she's still breech at thirty-six weeks, he suggests a more aggressive approach called an external cephalic version. An ECV is a procedure in which they try to manually flip the baby.

The procedure is done at the hospital. We're informed we'll need to follow a specific protocol because of a new virus everyone is worried about: COVID-19. My mom has mentioned the virus to me a few times so I'm not completely unfamiliar, but until now I hadn't given it much thought.

We arrive at Winnie Palmer at 4:00 a.m. We're handed masks when we approach the front door. They take our temperature and ask us to sanitize our hands. This seems very serious and I start to think maybe my mom is right to be alarmed.

They prep me by sanitizing my entire body. They disinfect my nasal passages and mouth and put me in a paper gown and hair net.

When I get back to our curtained cubby in triage, I feel unprepared for the upcoming procedure and nervous. Dr. Bartfield and his partner, Dr. Mervis, show up shortly after and help calm me down. The anesthesiologist arrives to place the epidural, which is supposed to relax me and block the pain. This totally backfires. During the procedure, when they start to try to flip her, I go into an extreme panic. It had not occurred to me that I wouldn't be able to feel my baby moving anymore. I can't stand it. I spiral very quickly so Dr. Mervis decides it's best for me and Isla if they don't continue. When the epidural wears off and I calm down, they explain we're likely looking at a C-section delivery. Dr. Mervis says kindly, "Sometimes there's a reason they won't flip."

> THE MEDICATIONS I AM STILL ON RULE ALL OF MY OPTIONS OUT. I WOULDN'T BE ADMITTED AT A BIRTHING CENTER AND NO DOCTOR THAT I'VE COME ACROSS WOULD ATTEMPT A BREECH BIRTH WITH A MOTHER ON BLOOD THINNERS.

A C-section is certainly not what I had in mind. It seems like a cruel twist that after so many miscarriages, so many years, and so much upward battle, I won't be allowed to have a vaginal birth. I am very disappointed, tender, and bruised. But I am resigned. The medications I am still on rule all of my options out. I wouldn't be admitted at a birthing center and no doctor that I've come across would attempt a breech birth with a mother on blood thinners.

The following day, Dr. Vidali tells me he is worried about COVID-19 and is advising his patients to quarantine if they are actively taking immune suppressants and/or pregnant. I am both. He wants to take every precaution and as the days unfold, I realize he is completely right to be concerned. So I started maternity leave early. We pull Jolene out of school because the risk of her contracting the virus is high. We start homeschooling, have groceries delivered, and only leave the house for mandatory doctor appointments. It is absolutely terrifying, alienating, and exhausting. As if a high-risk, breech pregnancy isn't enough to worry about, now we are contending with a full-blown pandemic that lists pregnancy as a risk factor. Can you be doubly high-risk?

Homeschooling is a crazy hard transition for everyone.

Jolene is scared and upset. She's confused. Clay is overwhelmed. We try to keep things in perspective but we're all in uncharted waters.

All of my doctors initiate emergency policies. Support people are no longer allowed at appointments. All non-essential appointments are canceled or rescheduled. Tons of my friends have egg retrievals or even IVF transfers canceled. "Elective" surgeries for things like endometriosis or fibroids are canceled. Hospitals all over the world stop allowing anyone into the birthing or even recovery room. I am worried that Clay won't be allowed to be with us when Isla is born. I am scared for myself but mostly sad for him.

At my next appointment—still deemed essential—with the MFM, he decides it is time for Isla to be born. He doesn't want to test my immune system's resilience anymore and advises Dr. Bartfield that we should deliver at thirty-eight weeks. He assures me that my baby is fine and at this point, she's safer out than in. I agree and drive across town to see Dr. Bartfield. We do a stress test and he agrees with Dr. Fuentes's assessment. It's the end of March and I can see the finish line.

WITHIN A MATTER OF DAYS I'LL HOLD THIS CHILD THAT I'VE BEEN FIGHTING FOR FOR ALMOST A DECADE.

Dr. Bartfield begins all the necessary paperwork and we schedule the surgery for April 2nd, 2020.

"We could do April 1st but then she'd be an April Fools' baby," he jokes. "I feel good about April 2nd, plus I'm working that day and I'd like to see this through," he continues.

The conversation feels surreal. Within a matter of days I'll hold this child that I've been fighting for for almost a decade.

"Do you have everything ready?" he asks.

"I do," I reply. "Car seat is installed and bags are packed." Holding my breath, I ask, "Is Winnie Palmer still allowing partners?"

"One person can accompany you, but whoever that is can't trade out. It has to be the same person for the entirety of the stay," he responds. "But I can't promise that won't change," he adds.

I'm not sure how to react to this so I sit silently with my lips pressed together.

"Bring him with you and we'll hope for the best," he says, noticing my anxious energy.

CHAPTER 13

Isla

TO THINK, I WAS FOOLISH ENOUGH TO BELIEVE
IT WAS I WHO NEEDED TO BIRTH HER.

On April 1st, 2020, we went for our last evening walk as a family of three. We walked slowly through our neighborhood and talked about everything and nothing. Jolene dominated the conversation with questions and fun facts about animals and nature. She talked about fishing and butterflies and soaked up our undivided attention. We've spent a lot of time over the last couple of months talking to her about the arrival of a baby. She's excited but also nervous. For so many years it didn't feel safe to talk to Jolene about siblings, so she's not really used to the idea. She only knows about one of the miscarriages and sometimes I wonder if she even remembers it. Once Isla is here safely, I'll be better able to talk to Jolene about everything I've been through. Jolene snaps some pictures of us smiling in front of the house. She loves to take pictures and the images show a very happy scene. I'll miss this belly.

We go to bed and I run through all the things I've done to try and get Isla to flip. All of the inversions, chiropractor appointments, acupuncture, even handstands in the pool. I say out loud to myself, "You did your best. I forgive you," and fall asleep for the last time with Isla as part of me. Tomorrow, I get to meet my baby.

On April 2nd, Clay and I arrived at Winnie Palmer Hospital. We pull into the multistory parking garage and when we step out of the car it hits me like a ton of bricks: I'm about to have a baby. We put our COVID masks on, grab our bags, lock the car, and head to the entrance. We pass through security and check in for a scheduled C-section. I am so incredibly relieved when they don't stop Clay from joining me. I grip his hand tightly and hope he can feel my elation. When we get to the receptionist, the hospital's COVID policy is explained: one support person, no switching out. Jolene won't be able to meet Isla until we're released. My heart sinks a little bit. I've imagined this moment so many times and feel slightly resentful that it won't play out the way I envisioned. But, as with all things over the last decade, nothing goes to plan. That's okay, I think.

We're directed to the surgery floor and wait to be called for

> *But, as with all things over the last decade, nothing goes to plan. That's okay, I think.*

prep. Protocol requires us to keep our masks on at all times and there are sanitizing stations everywhere. Hospitals always feel like cold, isolating places but these protocols make it even more so. Clay leans over to snap a picture of us, masks and all.

"Last picture of us before Isla arrives!" he beams.

Surgery prep is very similar to the prep we did a week ago for the attempted flip. A sort of trial run, if you will. I undress and stare at myself in the mirror before a nurse sanitizes me from head to toe. "Absolutely beautiful and so loved," I say to my belly, my baby. I regret not bringing my phone to snap one last picture, so I snap a mental image instead. I tell myself I'll never forget this moment—the moment my body overcame every imaginable obstacle and successfully carried my sixth pregnancy to term. Any fear I have about the C-section slips away and I feel capable of absolutely anything.

After I'm appropriately sanitized and gowned, I'm reunited with Clay. The anesthesiologist arrives and we discuss options. I explain my terrible reaction to the epidural, so she recommends a spinal block. I've done some research and I agree this is the way to go. Dr. Bartfield arrives and he's got a buddy with him—Dr. Mervis.

"Couldn't miss it," he says as he clasps my hand.

This is what support looks like. This is what medicine should look like. I am so incredibly honored.

"ABSOLUTELY BEAUTIFUL AND SO LOVED,"
I SAY TO MY BELLY, MY BABY.

They explain the procedure in detail and agree with the spinal block decision. Clay is instructed to wait outside while the anesthesiologist places the block. There's nothing more anxiety-inducing than being wheeled into surgery watching your person standing at a door that's swinging shut. I've seen this image too many times. *It's only for a moment*, I remind myself.

The spinal block truly does take a moment and isn't painful. I don't have any intense reaction and feel quite relaxed. They lay me back and people start to fill the room. I can hear Dr. Bartfield and Dr. Mervis chatting and it brings me a great sense of calm. They place the drape between me and my belly. Clay joins me right as I'm starting to wonder, *Where the heck is my husband?* He takes a seat by my left ear and I feel ready.

THEY PLACE HER ON MY CHEST AND SHE CALMS DOWN INSTANTLY. SO DO I.

There's a clear section in the drape that's covered by a flap. I stare at it intensely while I grip Clay's hand. I listen intently, trying to decipher the sounds on the other side. What feels simultaneously like an instant and an eternity passes and they fold down the flap. There she is. I can't take it in—I'm in utter disbelief that she's really here, safe, alive. They take my hands and press them to her through the plastic. I am completely overwhelmed by her presence. She's not clearing her airway sufficiently so they have to put her on oxygen. They inform us she will have to go to the NICU but they allow me to hold her first. They place her on my chest and she calms down instantly. So do I.

> MY LIFE HAS NEVER BEEN MORE
> BEAUTIFUL THAN THIS MOMENT.

It's hard to explain the emotion of meeting Isla after so much loss and such a scary pregnancy. It's a moment I have quite literally almost killed myself to achieve. I look at her and then look around as if for confirmation that it's not a dream this time. It's real. She's real. I doubt the nurses know what we've been through but the doctors certainly do. The sterile, cold room feels sacred in this moment. I feel no pain or fear anymore. What I feel can only be described as grace despite the grief.

After a few days in the hospital we are released. We head straight to pick up Jolene and she meets her baby sister for the first time. My life has never been more beautiful than this moment.

Isla proves to be everything I knew she would be: strong-willed, determined, and powerful beyond belief. As with Jolene, I know I will learn so much from her. *Isla, for me, was a reunion with the code of grace. She simultaneously showed me my fragility and strength. She showed me that, really, fragility and strength are one and the same.*

To think I was foolish enough to believe it was I who needed to birth her.

MY JOURNEY TO ISLA

2,111 days, 5 surgeries, 966 injections, 146 vials of blood taken, 15 IVs, 1 epidural, 1 spinal block, 1 C-section, 11 specialists.

Was it hard? Yes. Did it destroy me? Almost. Was it a gift? Absolutely.

PART II

This Is What Support Looks Like

CHAPTER 14

The Birth of Selah Fertility

When I was pregnant with Isla, I often felt crushing worry, but one word brought me instant calm: selah. It kept repeating in my mind like a beautiful melody. I wasn't familiar with the word and didn't actually recognize it as a word initially. I thought of it more as a sound like the universal "om." It brought me instant calm. I found I was able to slow things down when focusing on the sound. When I typed "selah" into Google, tons of results populated. The meaning is not entirely clear but it's thought to be an exclamation or musical direction that encourages us to pause and reflect. It could also mean "to lift up." When I read this, I about fell out of my chair.

Selah appears in the Hebrew Bible seventy-four times. It was a sign that was impossible to ignore. A culmination of all the grief, anguish, trials, hope, hard work, and healing I'd experienced over the last decade. It was as if God himself was saying, "Take a deep breath and trust." I became quite enamored with the concept of selah and, as I looked back on my life, realized selah was often what was missing.

Selah has become a way of life for me. Whenever I'm feeling overwhelmed, anxious, or upset, I lean on selah and remind myself to take pause. It grounds me in the present and also points me to the future.

※

With all the time I spend reading through online support groups, the desperate need for guidance is so clear. So many women are receiving completely incorrect information in these groups and, sadly, from their doctors. I truly believe that all advice given is well intended; however, so much of what I read is outdated and flat-out wrong. There are women in these groups having upward of twelve miscarriages. It's unfathomable. They believe—because their doctors have told them this—that they have gotten all of the necessary testing. They believe that they're doing everything they can.

But the medical system is failing them. They are not being told the whole story. Nobody is getting to the root of the problem. How on earth a doctor can allow a woman to have that many miscarriages without they themselves looking for an alternate solution is beyond me. I believe it is their ethical responsibility to read the current research but, clearly, these doctors are not doing that. They are throwing spaghetti at the wall hoping it sticks. The burden of care lands on the patient. The standard of care falls short.

How do I best support them? I wonder while I'm nursing Isla back to sleep. My friend, Kristyn, is pregnant and she recently hired a doula. *Aha*! I think. A doula is a person focused entirely on supporting women and couples. This is how I support them. I apply and sign up for a three-day doula education course in Jacksonville, Florida. It will be the first time I'm away from Isla even though she's a year and a half. Clay is out of town for work but my mom offers to watch the girls.

The course is fantastic. I'm surrounded by women committed to nurturing others and it's really moving. They share their stories and talk about how they came to be here. One of the participants is seventeen years old and wants to help teens navigate pregnancy. Another is a social worker and wants to provide more support for pregnant women in abuse shelters. When I share my reason for applying, I say boldly for the first time: "I want to help women get and stay pregnant." It feels really right. I go on to say I'd like to help women be more educated about their fertility options, their bodies, ways to support themselves through lifestyle, mindset, and nutrition. I heard something once that went something like "the strongest among us are the ones that survive the fire and turn back to pull others out." This implies choice when, for me, there isn't one. I know without a flicker of doubt that I will turn back. I know I will get down in the ashes with the women I support. I know I will bring water, shine light, and beg them to crawl out of the rubble.

There are things that I know for sure: I know I can help them. I know I can provide education, resources, support, community, compassion, clarity, and referrals. I also know that if I build it, they will come. The more I think about it, the more it starts to feel like a career path for me. I feel confident that this is something I can really do.

When I return home, I start compiling all the research I've done over the last decade and attempt to make it more approachable. Some of the topics, particularly the ones about the immune system and pregnancy, are overwhelming and complicated. I put together resources, information, guides, and a tremendous amount of educational content. A longtime friend of mine, Katie Mancilla, owns a referral-based digital marketing agency called KC Group Media. We jump on a call and I outline the general idea of what kind of company I'd like to build. Katie is a very straightforward person, so when she tells me she thinks it's a great idea I know she's not placating me. I also know that Katie is very busy, so when she shares that she is interested in helping me bring this idea to market I'm thrilled. She does some market research and proposes that her husband, Tony, help create the brand and website. When I agree to a call with the two of them, I don't realize that Tony supports some massively successful companies. He tells me point-blank that he isn't actively taking on new clients right now but he's so drawn to my idea that he wants to be part of it. He does have one caveat, though—that I won't water myself down. I can agree to that!

Together we formulate a support team for myself and for them—the couples that are lost. This process is very therapeutic for me. There are brand meetings, marketing meetings, PR meetings, and before long, consultations and clients.

The brand meetings are our starting point. Tony asks me to share imagery and brand content that resonates with me. We spend a lot of time talking through the concept and he highlights themes and adjectives that stand out as I'm describing my journey and my path forward. In the initial brand report, the words that stand out are: bold, proactive, personal. Tony puts together multiple visual presentations for me to review. They are beautiful and it's really hard to narrow it down to a favorite. The imagery and colors are bold and impactful. In the second stage of brand development, he presents the fonts and colors in an array of ways: on products, with iconography, in mock social media and website formats. We have primary fonts and colors along with secondary fonts and colors. The brand starts to really take form and it's shocking to me how well Tony captures the concept visually. Additional words start to emerge as important: graceful, honest, personalized. Tony tells me: "We've really identified your core values." He's so, so right.

As Tony is building out the website, Katie and I have lots of conversations around marketing. There are so many things to consider in such a fragile space. We talk through ways to be empathetic without being passive. If there's one thing I'm not, it's passive. I'm nervous about posting pictures on social media of pregnant women or even happy women. I worry this will be triggering for women struggling with infertility or miscarriage. Katie, thankfully, reminds me that a hopeful tone is the message we want to exude. Like Tony, she is so, so right. May I never be a woman afraid of the light and may I always surround myself with people that encourage me to overcome fear.

> *May I never be a woman afraid of the light and may I always surround myself with people that encourage me to overcome fear.*

"Think of Selah's social media as a virtual vision board," she says. I love it.

Katie and Tony work together to make sure everything is cohesive: the website, the social media, and the overall tone.

Katie launches Selah Fertility on Instagram and Facebook and we start posting content. Most of the information we put into the world is education-based. It is incredibly important to me that women know they have options. So many women say to me, "I've had all of the testing." But when I start asking about specific test results, they haven't been checked. Most of them have had base-level testing done and come to me with no tangible information. They have no actionable steps to take because nobody has done all of the necessary testing. Even if they have a more substantial set of tests, nobody has told them what to do in response to their results.

Within the website, we launch coaching programs for women at every stage of their fertility journey: trying to conceive, pregnant, or postpartum. We tailor our programs toward women who have struggled or are struggling with infertility, secondary infertility, miscarriage, recurrent miscarriage, or stillbirth. We also collaborate with Dr. Vidali to include comprehensive immunological testing, and we offer hormonal testing, male factor sperm testing, and telehealth OB-GYN services. Selah Fertility's message is centered around proactivity, self-advocacy, and the refusal to accept "unexplained" as a diagnosis. We leave no stone unturned and we attract clients that are ready to heal. Women approach me through every imaginable modality. They message me on Facebook, Instagram, and LinkedIn.

Tony recommends I offer a complimentary consultation

so that I can streamline the questions and requests. We add an option to instantly book a fifteen-minute consultation on the website. At the same time, Katie begins running ads on Google. Within four days of running the ads, I have four consults booked. I'm encouraged. My first consult stands me up and my elation bursts like a bubble. I'm so bummed. I sit myself down for a serious pep talk and remind myself that not everyone is ready to start this process. The fact that she booked a consult was probably a huge step for her. I just have to keep showing up and providing a safe space for connection. My mantra becomes: I am attracting clients that are ready to change their narrative.

My second consult (or first, depending on how you look at it) is with a woman experiencing secondary infertility. Her doctor has recommended that she get "injections to get pregnant" and she's asking me what that means. I have a hard time hiding my reaction and I tell her, honestly, he could mean several things. I ask if she recalls him discussing a procedure or treatment plan. She tells me that all he said was she "couldn't get pregnant without injections."

I feel the need to apologize for this doctor's behavior, but I don't because it's not mine to own. I can see the frustration, confusion, and pain in this woman's face and it reminds me exactly why I'm doing this.

"I am here for you," I say. "I can help you gain understanding about your options."

Secondary infertility is a strange, alienating experience. You don't quite fit in with the infertility community because many people don't sympathize with you. They often react in anger at your wish to have another child and say cruel things like "You should just be happy with the child you have." This is their pain speaking.

You feel a tremendous amount of shame because you don't want anyone to think you're not "happy enough" with your living child. A calling for a child is not something a person chooses. It's a deep, biological urge that one cannot snuff out. You can certainly choose not to pursue another child, but you cannot choose not to desire another child. It's also very challenging to navigate taking care of a child in the midst of experiencing infertility and/or miscarriage.

I arm this client with a list of questions for her doctor and some information on possible procedures he may have been suggesting. When she exits the video chat, I say a little prayer. I hope that she finds the answers she needs and, if not, I hope she allows me to support her.

Fertility can become an obsession. We seek a sense of control over our bodies because we feel we have lost control over the thing that matters most to us: our ability to have a child. We are steered toward compulsive behavior like charting our body temperature daily, watching for changes in our cervical mucous, tracking our menstrual cycles, monitoring our glucose levels, timing intercourse, signing up for every webinar, and taking every supplement touted as good for egg quality. At some point, we have to ask ourselves:

Does this support my overall wellness?

Does this contribute positively toward my goals?

We have to make sure what we're committing to actually feels aligned and makes sense for *us*. If acupuncture gives you anxiety, stop getting acupuncture! If charting every single detail of your cycle feels overwhelming, stop! We must fall in love with the process of becoming ourselves. Find what brings you joy and do that. Find what makes you feel safe and do that.

Our bodies cannot function well in a state of fear, stress, fight, fright, or freeze. *Trauma response looks different from person to person. We all react differently to a triggering event based on the environment we grew up in, our individual personalities, and our current emotional level of intelligence.* It is imperative to our well-being and, as an extension, our fertility, that we calm and regulate our central nervous system. From this place we can bring forth life.

Don't get me wrong—if you're reading this book, I know it's not as simple as this for you. You likely need a ton of support and potentially medical interventions. I get it because I needed that too. But my soul also needed to let go and give it over to a higher power. I had to create my team, trust them, do my best, and leave the rest. I had to create a habit out of the concept of selah.

We have power in how we view our situation and our journey.

It's easy to forget that creating and sustaining life isn't just science. There's a lot of magic required too. Our thoughts matter, our words matter, how we approach something matters. We have power in how we view our situation and our journey.

We look back with gratitude and forward with wonder.

CHAPTER 15

Infertility: Colossal Crisis or Monumental Opportunity?

In March of 2022 I am attending a virtual conference on infertility that poses the question: Is it a colossal crisis or a monumental opportunity? My initial reaction is that it's both. The webinar is hosted by Julia Indichova, author of *The Fertile Female*, and I'm looking forward to interacting with her via Zoom. She writes in advance to attendees to encourage questions, so I jot a few down before clicking "Join meeting now."

Julia begins by introducing herself and then invites everyone to "unmute" and "say hello!" As you can imagine, the overlap is overwhelming, but Julia seems to receive a lot of energy from the moment. *Hmmm*, I think, *I still have work to do*.

After the initial introduction she leads us through some deep breathing exercises. I find my calm rather quickly after the "hello" assault. We are instructed to identity first our thoughts then our feelings.

My thought: *Do I want another baby?*
My feeling: fear.

"Give yourself permission to fully receive your feelings. Fully feel how alive you are!" Julia interrupts my spiral. "You can choose how to use your life force. The breath knows how to come in the same way a baby knows how to come in," she says.

As she leads into some movement exercises, I wonder, *Did I sign up for this class to gain knowledge or to gain clarity?* This is heavy right off the bat. When I tune back in, Julia is asking us to write down whatever feels like a crisis in our lives right now. It takes me some time to articulate it, but slowly it dawns on me that my crisis is fear of the unknown. I like to plan things and I struggle when I don't know the plan or the plan goes awry.

As if she knew my thoughts, she said, "We must receive the truth regardless of what the truth is."

What is my current truth? In my present moment, my truth is that I am exhausted. It becomes clear to me why I am here: self-care. I need to reconnect to myself in order to know what I need and, eventually, what I want. I most consistently practiced self-care when I was preparing for conception. I am repeating old patterns, revisiting old haunts. This is where I can become the best version of myself—in the space dedicated to healing. These are my people. I am recreating a community that I miss. A community of women fighting for their babies.

Some of the other women share feelings about what they're struggling with that are all too familiar to my experience of recurrent miscarriage: inability to trust the process, letting go, despair, grief, lack of support, sadness, searching for answers, pressure, acceptance, uncertainty, loneliness, isolation, and direction.

I turn my camera off as the tears start to flow freely down my cheeks. My reaction is always the same when I encounter a woman who is hurting—I wish that I could hold her hands in mine and guide her through the work.

> *We must decide if we will be victimized by our circumstance or become co-creators of our lives.*

The work seems so simple to type out here for you, but in reality, the work is the hardest thing you'll ever do. It will reward you in ways you can't imagine, though. We must decide if we will be victimized by our circumstance or become co-creators of our lives. Our power is in how we view and react to the situation. We must choose a journey of defeat or a journey filled with meaning and growth. We cannot escape the truth and we must decide to show up and fight for what we want. The fighter lives on.

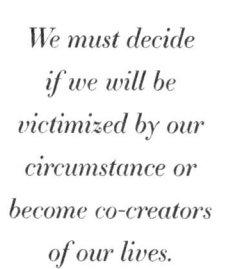

We should always honor love lost. We should always work toward transparency, growth, and healing. We should always shelve our expectations and embrace each other with grace, acceptance, and kindness.

CHAPTER 16

A Model for Supportive Medicine: The Endometriosis Summit

In 2022, I took part in a three-day conference dedicated to connecting patients and practitioners to discuss the devastating impact endometriosis can have on a woman's mental, physical, emotional, and social well-being. I wanted to attend this conference for several reasons, but mainly because I think it's imperative that practitioners are open to conversation with patients. The model of this conference is groundbreaking—people struggling with disease are put in a room with top experts who lead educational presentations on the topic. Most importantly, they allow for tons of Q and A. They have simultaneously created a platform for patient experience which allows them to build compassion and understanding into their practice.

Endometriosis is a disease I suffered from for years that ravaged my fertility. I want to gain as much information about the disease as possible for my current and future clients. I also want to attend to support Dr. Andrea Vidali, my reproductive immunologist and endometriosis excision surgeon.

On the morning of the conference, I'm up at 6:00 a.m., as I always am on weekdays. It's February of 2022. The sun isn't up yet, so when I wake the room is totally dark with the exception of the light emitted by a small blue night-light. I always wake before my alarm and silence it before it has the chance to chime and wake Isla. We co-sleep and, although I can't fully see her, I can feel her warmly snuggled into me. I listen to the rise and fall of her breath for a few moments before I slide out from underneath the blanket. She rolls over onto her back and lets out a long sigh. I throw on my sweatpants and jumper, grab my slippers, and head toward Jolene's room. The white-noise machine covers the creaking wood floor underfoot as I exit the room.

Jolene is sprawled across the bed with her left arm hanging off the mattress. She has a full-sized bed; however, she seems to suddenly take up all of the available space. Her hundreds of stuffed animals, which she calls "stuffies," are strewn around the bed and many have ended up on the floor. I step over flamingos, dragons, and bunnies as I softly say, "Good morning, Jolene."

She grumbles but doesn't open her eyes. Like her dad, she's not a morning person, and it takes at least twenty minutes to coax her out of bed. I turn off the bedroom fan and swing open her closet door to flood the room with light. "I'm freezing!" she protests. "The light is blinding me," she complains.

Her school uniform is laid out on the bed ready to tackle

another day of science labs, recess, and the cafeteria. Somehow it has avoided being kicked to the floor by Jolene's long limbs and is exactly where I placed it the night before.

"Please try not to wake Isla yet," I plead as she twists into a blanket burrito.

> AS I SWALLOW, I THINK ABOUT ALL THE WOMEN WHO DON'T KNOW LITTLE TIPS LIKE THIS. WOMEN TOTALLY UNFAMILIAR WITH HOW TO PROPERLY SUPPORT THEMSELVES. I WISH, NOT FOR THE FIRST TIME, THAT I COULD REACH OUT MY HAND TO EACH OF THEM.

Downstairs, I start to make breakfast and pack lunch for Jolene. While Clay is away for work, I serve hard-boiled eggs, fruit, yogurt, and bagels for breakfast. He makes omelets with ham, spinach, and cheese. I've tried to make an omelet but it always ends up more of a frittata, which Jolene turns her nose up at and pushes toward the sink. Hard-boiled eggs are fine, I remind myself.

I put the water on to boil and make myself a cup of tea. While the kettle heats up, I take out a jar of sprouted, raw, organic almond butter and eat two spoonfuls. Eating something high in fat and protein after waking is a habit I started while preparing to conceive. It's a habit I'll likely continue for the rest of my life as a way of supporting my blood sugar and my hormones. As I swallow, I think about all the women who don't know little tips like this. Women totally unfamiliar with how to properly support themselves. I wish, not for the first time, that I could reach out my hand to each of them.

I'm snapped out of my thoughts by Jolene thudding down the stairs. Before she makes it to the landing, Isla starts crying out. By the time I get to her, Jolene is already cuddling her. I overhear her tell Isla, "It's okay, you're not alone!" and my heart melts. They have each other. Neither of them is alone. I feel the gratitude bubble up inside and any annoyance I had about Jolene waking Isla up fades away.

Within the hour, I drop Jolene off. I drive home with Isla and my mom arrives as I'm cleaning up the morning's breakfast plates. She's going to look after Isla so I can help Dr. Sallie Sarrel set up for The Endometriosis Summit, which is being held in my hometown. We haven't met in person but she's felt like a friend and ally for the last six months. I'm excited to meet her and support her. When I arrive at the conference site, I'm greeted by Sallie, her dad, and both of their dogs. Sallie embraces me and immediately jumps into conversation about our aligned missions. Never a fan of small talk, I'm overjoyed by her intensity and authenticity.

We get to work setting up the room and unpacking tons of pamphlets and products she has brought for the attendees. She reviews the audio-visual presentations and run of the show. Dr. Andrea Vidali calls to say he's en route from New York via Miami. He arrives shortly after and his excitement is contagious. Sallie seems to relax now that Dr. Vidali is by her side. We jump on social media to do some last-minute outreach and I'm so honored to be able to support, in even the smallest of ways, this man who changed my life forever.

The next day kicks off early with an endometriosis excision surgery streamed live. When I arrive two hours after it begins, the surgery is still ongoing. I slip into the room and take a seat in the back row. Dr. Vidali is on stage moderating the surgery and giving a tremendous amount of insight to the spectators. The room is composed of surgeons, ob-gyns, pelvic floor therapists, advocates, and patients. You can spot the surgeons right away by their posture and heightened attention to detail on the screen. The patients sit with their notebooks open, jotting down questions or observations.

As I watch, I feel a sense of connection to the woman undergoing surgery. I never see her face, only her internal abdomen, but still I feel comradery. I wonder what challenges she has faced because of this disease. Does she struggle with infertility, miscarriage, pain? Is this her first surgery? Will she need future surgeries? I hope, to myself, that she has the support she needs to face whatever she's dealing with.

As the day progresses the energy increases. Dr. Vidali sits with me and we whisper back and forth about ideas and initiatives. In close proximity to him it's possible to feel his energy. I'm reminded of the first time I met Dr. Jeffery Braverman, and I realize that these men are driven by the same unrelenting urge to find solutions. As Dr. Vidali bustles back and forth from the microphone to the stage and back to the chair next to me, he manages to fill the entire room not only with his passion but with his compassion. As I continue to draw parallels between Dr. Vidali and Dr. Braverman, I find myself praying that Dr. Vidali rests. A passion like that can be all-consuming, and in order to keep it burning one must rest. Everyone in the room is drawn to him. Everyone wants a piece of him. It's like a magnet pulling the entire building to one small pinnacle.

After lunch there is a panel on fertility. It starts by acknowledging that fertility can be highly triggering for a person with endometriosis. Most of these women have struggled or are struggling with infertility or miscarriage. A handful of them have lost their reproductive organs to the disease or a hysterectomy-happy surgeon. There is a tremendous amount of tension surrounding the topic. Most of the patients perk up and edge forward in their seats. Is it anticipation or anxiety? That is yet to be determined.

The question posed is "Is treating fertility in the person with endometriosis as simple as excision surgery?" and the panel is led by Dr. Vidali. He explains the relevance of the conversation and allows people a moment to remove themselves from the room if the topic is too painful for them. Nobody leaves. Fertility, he says, is like the elephant in the room. With emotion thick in his voice, he says that often the opportunity of biological parenthood has been taken away by this disease.

Sallie encourages me to go to the front of the room so that I may record the conversation. I practically knock my chair over at the suggestion and rush forward. As I walk to the front, I see many people also recording. From experience I know that traumatizing material often doesn't absorb even when we so desperately want to know the information. I picture these women playing back the videos when they're back home curled up in bed. No doubt they'll be frantically taking notes and hoping for a statement so explosive that it cuts directly to the core of their questions.

I bend down and sit on my knees. I like it here, up front. I wish I'd arrived earlier so I could be here all day.

"I hate dogma," Dr. Vidali states boldly. "One of them is that IVF can bypass endometriosis." Immediately, I'm reminded of the many doctors who dismissed my concern that I had endometriosis based on the fact that I could get pregnant naturally.

"How do you feel about IVF first?" he asks the audience. He's talking about the standard of using IVF prior to addressing endometriosis. "This is the current state of things," he says. "I don't like these algorithms which lock people in."

The presentation continues and my legs start to go numb. I shuffle onto my butt and feel the blood rush back to my feet.

"We know the incidence of endometriosis in severe fertility cases is very high," he shares. "No matter what you do, one out of eight good prognosis couples who are doing IVF have recurrent implantation failure." I feel his energy shift to frustration. He's getting angry. "This is why endometriosis and the immune system—and they go together—need to be analyzed. It needs to be addressed."

I consider standing up to cheer out loud and clap wildly. But I stay seated. I'm glued to every word. He's speaking my story.

He brings up inflammation and progesterone. I can barely contain myself.

"Doctors are obliged to troubleshoot," he says loudly.

I choke back tears. I clench my jaw. I exhale slowly through my nose. I feel validated.

He ends by stating that excision surgery that removes endometriosis can improve fertility by decreasing inflammation. He adds that often what he sees clinically after IVF does not reflect the clinical studies. And this opens a new can of worms.

Sallie chimes in. She announces that they will be hosting a fertility conference in October and the room erupts in applause. It looks like what I observed in the attendees was indeed anticipation.

For three days we gather together for panel-led discussions, interviews, and even interactive sessions. Each session allows for questions from both practitioners and patients. It's unlike any conference I've attended. I can't think of any other scenario in which patients have direct access to speak with world-renowned doctors, authors, and experts so candidly.

On Saturday evening I'm invited to attend a dinner for the staff, speakers, and doctors. Sallie insists and I agree to join in. There is a dynamic that usually exists between patient and doctor that puts the patient at a disadvantage. Given that, I wonder if the dinner will be uncomfortable. Will I feel as if I'm waiting for my ob-gyn to enter the room and start asking questions? *At least I'm in a dress and not a paper gown*, I think.

I walk in and find a family atmosphere. I look around and realize that a lot of the attendees have brought their spouses and some have even brought their children. It's not intimidating at all! I'm so relieved.

The bartender is serving up Aperol Spritzes in honor of Dr. Vidali's home country of Italy. A lovely touch orchestrated by Sallie. She grabs one for herself and encourages me to do the same. Then she introduces me to a group of women who practice pelvic floor therapy. They are warm, welcoming, and full of fun. The hotel staff are busy setting up the food stations and people start drifting toward dinner plates.

THIS IS WHAT SUPPORT LOOKS LIKE. THIS IS WHAT ADVOCACY LOOKS LIKE. THIS IS WHAT MEDICINE CAN LOOK LIKE.

All around the room I overhear conversations about patient experience and ways to educate people about the effects of endometriosis. I stand for a moment, cocktail in hand, and take it in. This is what support looks like. This is what advocacy looks like. This is what medicine can look like. These people are at the top of their game but they're still so open to learning and expanding. They want to improve themselves for their patients. It's incredible to witness.

The final day of the summit includes a tribute to Dr. Jeffrey Braverman. I didn't expect to become emotional but I sit next to Mrs. Vidali with silent tears sliding down my cheeks. Dr. Vidali is on stage alone. *He is just one man*, I think to myself before he begins speaking. One man that is making such a vast impact on so many people. It's incredibly inspiring. It encourages me to keep going. It reminds me that I can make a difference.

He starts by sharing some background on himself. He attended Columbia University and was originally trained as a reproductive endocrinologist. Then he leads into an introduction of Dr. Braverman. He shares what I already knew: that the man was a genius and, at the time, was the youngest graduate from NYU when he was around sixteen. He also shares that Dr. Braverman inspired him to study immunology and how it relates to fertility and pregnancy.

"One important observation is that the transition between the state of health and the state of disease is not a line. Health and disease are a gradient transition. It's a process. You become sick. It didn't happen overnight. One of the failures of medicine is to miss the graduality," he says.

As he's speaking, I flash back to the red-flag list I filled out four years ago.

"The majority of people with endometriosis experience reproductive problems as well. Some don't have pain; we call that 'silent' endometriosis. The only symptom is the infertility or the pregnancy loss. People tell them, 'Keep on trying, you will succeed.' But the reality is that the time to pregnancy after a pregnancy loss is up to five years. Sometimes people don't have five years," he continues.

Again, I have the urge to jump from my seat and cheer him on. Preach!!!

"Never accept 'unexplained' as a reason. I think there is an obligation to at least try to find the answer. Having to look at the immune system is very important."

And there it is. The whole truth of it. I think back to myself ten years ago and wish that girl could have heard this presentation. I think about all the women who still need to hear this information.

Selah, I think to myself. *Advocacy, support, education.*

As the conference comes to a close, Dr. Vidali asks me to join him in presenting for his upcoming reproductive immunology summit. Honored is an understatement.

REIKI

I've started working with a reiki master. I felt drawn to her long before I physically met her. I've known, for a long time, that she walks alongside me. We orbit each other through a couple of degrees of separation for a few months before I actually make an appointment. We have lots of similar friends and Kat often appears on my social media timelines at events I decided to skip at the last minute, or she pops into a coffee shop I left a couple of hours prior. She offers in-person or distance services but I want to be as close as possible to her. All of the most important people in my life make me wait. They inadvertently (or purposefully) show me that we can't plan anything. They show me that everything happens in due time. And sometimes, they show me that time doesn't exist.

Kat lets me know that she can't see me at the time I booked. She reschedules for several hours later and, although I'm disappointed, I agree. This shift in my schedule opens up two free hours for me, and as a result I get to spend some time with my husband without the kids. It's so nice to adult together. So nice, in fact, that I end up being late for my appointment with Kat because I wait until the last minute to leave and then I hit traffic. This is very out of character for me. Nevertheless, I arrive in a great mood and when she apologizes for the change in schedule, I'm able to genuinely assure her that it was a blessing to me.

"Time is subjective, anyway. You're here at the right time," she says casually.

continued

And I know, deep in my heart, she's absolutely right. The room where she practices is full of beautiful things. She has hung unique, powerful artwork on the walls and has plants placed throughout the room. I lie down comfortably on her table and she hands me a squishy llama toy with its head hanging off.

"This is stress llama," she tells me as she continues to prepare herself.

"His head is hanging off," I observe out loud just in case she hasn't noticed.

"Telling," she says with a smile.

This poor llama has seen a lot, I think.

The next hour is both energizing and relaxing simultaneously. Kat moves around me very slowly but it's as if she has some kind of magnetic force within her. Almost as if she's buzzing. She's mostly silent with the exception of a few occasional deep exhales. I drift in and out of light sleep and seem to float between reality and a dream. It's easy, in this place, to lose track of which is which.

Kat quietly lets me know she's finished and invites me to open my eyes slowly. When I do, she looks so incredibly alive.

"How do you feel?" she asks excitedly.

"I feel wonderful!" I reply sleepily.

Over the next half hour, she shares with me everything she felt and it all resonates very deeply. She is so encouraging and positive. We talk about energy and how it impacts others. We talk about intention and how it's one of the first impressions people get from us. She tells me that during our session it was as if the whole world, the entire universe, and any higher power imaginable was cheering me on.

"Keep going," she says. "Do the hard shit."

When I leave, I call my husband. He says right away, "Babe, I feel like we've just walked out of a fog." *Maybe we did*, I think. It's fascinating to me to hear him say that, as he wasn't in the room with us. Shoot, he didn't even know I was attending a reiki session. Nevertheless, it seems he felt some kind of impact as my energy shifted. As if he could sense that my vision had become clearer.

I decide then that I'd like to work with Kat on a personal and professional level. I believe that her encouraging energy will be vastly helpful to the women I'm honored to work with. I ask her if she'd like to meet soon to discuss the possibility and she agrees.

We meet a couple of weeks later halfway between her house and mine. I'm early, per usual, and she's late, per usual. I smirk to myself as I recognize this pattern in my life and realize I no longer find it annoying but quite endearing. The universe loves to remind me that patience truly is a virtue.

When she sits down across from me, it's like seeing an old friend. Or perhaps even looking in the mirror. Hello, Ally. I take note that it has become easier for me to trust and be open. I am so filled with self-love about this shift. I almost knock the table over in delight. I want to trust her and this is such a huge marker of all the healing I've done.

continued

I don't do small talk well and apparently neither does Kat. She launches into a conversation about revealing the feminine divine.

By the time I check my phone, it's been two hours and I'm officially running late for my next meeting. Touché, universe. I see you and I am softening daily.

I book two distance reiki sessions over the next two months. Kat is consistently a beam of light. When we get off the phone, I feel lighter and full of ease. Her unyielding message is that God, the universe, whatever you want to call a higher energy, has my back. Five years ago I wouldn't have been able to be onboard with this. I would have railed against the notion and listed all the contradictory evidence. Now, as I look back over all the ups and downs of the last decade, I smile, and I believe it's true.

CHAPTER 17

Knowledge and Grace

THERE ARE MOMENTS IN WHICH I STILL THINK I'M DREAMING SHE'S MINE. GRIEF IS NOT LINEAR.

I am planning Isla's second birthday celebration and it's bringing up a lot of emotions. The trauma of so many miscarriages and pregnancy after loss still lingers. There were moments in which I wasn't sure I'd ever hold her in my arms. There are moments in which I still think I'm dreaming she's mine. Grief is not linear.

A huge part of my healing was forgiving myself. My inner dialogue was so aggressive and angry. Especially when I finally got some answers about what was causing the miscarriages. I kept thinking, on loop, that things could have been so different if only I had known about reproductive immunology sooner.

It would have changed your whole trajectory, I hear myself thinking as I try to fall asleep.

You might have had only one miscarriage, as I check out at the grocery store.

If only you'd known, when I'm waiting for the water to boil.

Those "what ifs" can break your heart a million times over. These patterns took a tremendous amount of dismantling. Therapy. Sitting in the moment and allowing myself to be really, really angry.

Something that really helped me get these emotions up and out was creating what I like to call "controlled chaos." I'd create a scene in a safe place. For example, I'd fill a large bowl with ice cubes and throw them onto a noisy surface. I really liked dumping the entire bowl into my empty bathtub. Stomping on empty aluminum cans, shaking a can with pennies in it, screaming into my pillow, punching a soft target, shredding up paper—simple things that provided instant relief.

When I wasn't home these methods obviously weren't an option, so this became my go-to: Breathe in, breathe out. Say to yourself: "I did the best I could with the knowledge and awareness I had in the moment."

It was effective. I felt compassion and kindness toward myself instead of fury. Sometimes I still employ this mantra, because there's never a day that goes by without me thinking about the miscarriages. I spend time every day thinking of what we've lost and what we've gained as a result. I pray for the sisters I have found along this path. And, every day, I work through my grief, turn my face toward the light, and thank God for miracles (wherever they may be).

Actionable steps for overcoming miscarriage:

- Allow yourself to feel all of the emotions that bubble up.
- Be patient with yourself (and ask for patience from others).
- Lean on your support system.
- Join a support group and consider a fertility coach or doula.
- When you're ready, demand extensive testing. Make sure this includes a complete semen analysis, full thyroid panel and, if you've had more than one miscarriage, consider reproductive immunology testing.
- Review test results with your doctor and ask for a "next steps" plan.
- Take action to address any red flags within the test results.
- Consider spending three months focusing on improving egg and sperm quality before trying to conceive again.
- Remember that grief is not linear. There is no timeline.

By the time most women find me through Selah Fertility, they're heartbroken. They're exhausted, angry, bitter, confused, and incredibly sad. They're raw. Most of them have been told terrible things like—

"You're too old."

"You have terrible egg quality."

"Maybe a baby isn't part of God's plan for you."

"At least you . . ."

Most of them have been struggling with infertility or recurrent pregnancy loss for years. Some of them have had upward of five IVF cycles. When they look in the mirror, words like "failure" come to mind. They are so incredibly resilient. They carry trauma with them daily.

Finding a sense of calm in the midst of grief is like stepping into the eye of a hurricane. It's quiet, slow, and peaceful; but the storm rages all around. You can feel the threat at the edges, bleeding into the calm, tickling the fray. Some people handle grief by talking constantly. Some people escape every chance they get. Others cry in the corner. Some latch onto each other tightly. Others silently observe the chaos.

Trauma response is unique to each person. Like the opposite of a love language—two sides of the same coin. We grieve and cope in our own ways. No response is wrong. Nobody can tell another how to grieve. Nobody can put terms on our process. There are, however, ways in which we can improve our coping mechanisms. Ways in which we can respond to ourselves and each other with more compassion and love.

> *Our thoughts become our reality. Our emotions emit vibrations that impact all of our cells.*

The first thing we work on is mindset. We change the narrative slowly until it becomes a habit. "I'm a failure" becomes "I'm doing my best. I'm showing up for myself."

Mindset is often debated in fertility. People say things like "You can't manifest a baby." Here's my take: A healthy mindset is the cornerstone of success in any situation. Fertility is no exception. Do people get pregnant without a healthy mindset? Absolutely. Do people stay pregnant without a healthy mindset? Yes. Does that mean we can skip over the mindset work? Definitely not. Our thoughts become our reality. Our emotions emit vibrations that impact all of our cells.

As part of our mindset work, we explore trauma response and grief management. Not everyone responds to trauma in the same way. It's important to understand the individual response to specific triggers.

Mindset is ongoing work. It's not something we address, master, and move on. It's something we have to be constantly aware of and consistently tweak. The goal is to be kinder to ourselves. I want to be very clear that masking emotions with false or toxic positivity is not the goal here. A healthy mindset allows for all emotions to bubble up and be felt, honored, and released.

IF THERE IS ONLY ONE TAKEAWAY THAT I HOPE YOU ABSORB, IT'S THAT YOU ARE WILDLY CAPABLE.

There are many methods that can help with mindset. A lot of which I discussed in this book. Things like meditation, therapy, yoga, journaling, support groups, sound baths, time with loved ones, guided visualization, affirmations, or even an Epsom salt bath.

With a strong mindset comes the capacity to self-advocate. It's very hard to stand up for yourself when you're in a place of victimization, shame, and vulnerability. So along with changing the self-dialogue we work on dialogue with everybody else; particularly our practitioners.

Through education and support I embolden women to get the right testing, challenge the standard of care, and seek out partnerships that support them rather than deplete them. Education is a huge part of Selah Fertility.

Understanding our fertility and our bodies in addition to understanding how things like endometriosis, inflammation, our immune systems, and nutrition can impact them is vitally important to our overall well-being. If we have to work this hard to become mothers, surely we should want to be the best mothers we can be by showing up as healthy, healed versions of ourselves. If we can heal our own bodies and minds, we set the stage for healthy relationships with our children. It's also incredibly empowering to truly understand your body and be able to support it.

If you know what tests to get, you can also know what results are optimal. Once we know that, doctors can't overlook or dismiss us. We're able to converse with them on a more even playing field.

I am now on the "other side" of recurrent pregnancy loss.

Isla turned two yesterday. Jolene turns ten next month. I have launched Selah Fertility and I'm helping multiple women a week approach preconception, pregnancy, birth, and motherhood with knowledge and grace.

There are still days when the grief overtakes me, days where I have to crawl into bed and shut the blinds. There are still nights when I wake up at 2:00 a.m. panicking that I'm pregnant or not pregnant or that something bad is going to happen to my children. Sometimes I still feel phantom kicks in my womb and I feel excitement and anxiety simultaneously. Occasionally a baby shower invitation or a pregnancy announcement still triggers me. Sometimes a well-meaning stranger will ask, "You going to try for a boy soon?" And I have to weigh my response carefully. But most days I feel balanced, healed, and at peace.

> GRIEF IS NOT LINEAR. IT COMES AND GOES AND OFTEN SNEAKS UP ON ME WHEN I LEAST EXPECT IT.

I do things differently now. I put emphasis on things that bring me joy, make me feel safe, and don't exhaust me. I've learned to say no. I take time to pause and reflect as the concept of selah has become habit.

Grief is not linear. It comes and goes and often sneaks up on me when I least expect it. At the stroke of midnight on New Year's Eve, for example, or when Clay and I finally manage to squeeze in a date night, and he steps away to use the bathroom. What I can promise you though is, although it never goes away, it does get less raw, less heavy.

∽

If there is only one takeaway that I hope you absorb, it's that you are wildly capable. Your ability to heal is greater than anyone has permitted you to believe. You are capable because I am capable and, like I said in the beginning, you and I are the same. I hope you get everything you've ever dreamed of. I hope you learn to trust yourself again. I am rooting for you.

Gratitude and Acknowledgments

It is not lost on me that Isla would not be here without a host of people. My words fall short.

Dr. Andrea Vidali—you are truly a miracle worker. Thank you for believing in me when I didn't believe in myself. Thank you for dedicating your life to hearing women, healing women, and bringing forth many miracles.

Dr. Jeffrey Braverman—you are missed every day. Thank you for creating a world in which "unexplained" wasn't acceptable. Thank you for fighting for me even from your deathbed.

Dr. Michael McNichol—thank you for trusting me and opening your mind to my host of challenges. Thank you for supporting me every single day.

Dr. Michael Bartfield—thank you for going above and beyond to support me. Thank you for always ordering the extra lab work even when you knew it wasn't necessary. Thank you for allowing me to have ultrasounds whenever I felt unsure. You helped give me the strength to make it through.

Dr. Matthew Mervis—thank you for attempting an external

cephalic version. Thank you for assisting Dr. Bartfield in a flawless C-section when she wouldn't turn. Thank you for showing up.

Dr. Saima Bhatti—thank you for allowing me to let go.

Dr. Judi Addelston—thank you for listening to me for twenty years. Thank you for the wisdom. Thank you for helping me see what was right in front of me.

Carolyn Johnson—thank you for protecting my girls. Thank you for helping me hear them so clearly.

Aimee Raupp—thank you for providing such a safe and beautiful space for me to learn, share, and heal. Thank you for encouraging me to follow my heart. Thank you for sharing your light with so many.

Clay Fletcher—thank you for loving me so much and so well. You are the best husband, father, and man I know.

Jolene Fletcher—thank you for showing me that miracles are possible. You are the light of our lives.

Isla Fletcher—thank you for being patient with me. Thank you for staying. You are my reunion with the Code of Grace, my angel on earth.

Margaret Errington—thank you for being my safe harbor. Thank you for reminding me to pause and reflect. You were my selah.

Sylvia Errington—you have supported me in everything I have ever done. Thank you for encouraging me, believing in me, and showing me the power of a mother's love.

Adam Errington—thank you for stepping in every single time I needed you.

Keith Donnelley—thank you for always showing up.

Ruth, Philip, and Melissa Bigg—thank you for loving

our dreams as much as we did. Thank you for helping dreams become reality.

Simon Errington—you once said to me, "Now is the time for healing," and so it is.

Kristyn Gohlke—thank you for moving mountains to be by my side when I needed you the most. Thank you for witnessing my grief and my joy for the better part of a lifetime.

Christie McLeod—you've been my life buoy, my confidant, my sister. Thank you for always knowing exactly what to say. Thank you for praying for me and my babies every single day.

Beth Grossmann—thank you for believing in me, encouraging me, and listening to me. You always made sure I knew I wasn't alone.

Jill Schulte—thank you for your constant support and friendship. You were the first person that truly heard me. Your resilience continues to inspire me.

Karen Nitzsche—thank you for guiding me to Dr. Braverman. Without you, Isla wouldn't be here. You are the most selfless person I know. I count myself among the many women whose lives you have changed forever.

Kathy Pollard—your belief in me moved mountains. Thank you.

Aleksandra Clack—although you're an ocean away, I still feel you in waves. Thank you for holding my hand every step of the way.

Cortney Gibson—thank you for the endless support, advice, and laughter.

Katie and Tony Mancilla—thank you for believing in me. To the moon!

Dr. Christian Bolden—thank you for seeing me. Thank you for pushing me. Thank you for opening my eyes to the many ways in which we can serve others.

To the endless friends and family who shared kind words, support, and love—thank you.

To the women that have trusted me and allowed me to be part of their journey to motherhood, to support them during their pregnancies, and to be present to hold them during their births—it is an honor of the greatest magnitude. I will think of you and yours every day for the rest of my life.

To my team at Greenleaf Publishing—you made this so much easier than I could have imagined. Thank you for your compassion, grace, and professionalism. Sally Garland, thank you for being you. You encouraged me and understood me so beautifully.

Recommended Reading and Resources

Becoming Supernatural by Dr. Joe Dispenza

Body Belief by Aimee E. Raupp

Dirty Genes by Dr. Ben Lynch

Hormone Intelligence by Dr. Avia Romm

I Had a Miscarriage by Dr. Jessica Zucker

Ina May's Guide to Childbirth by Ina May Gaskin

Is Your Body Baby-Friendly? by Alan E. Beer, M.D.

Nurture by Erika Chidi Cohen

Real Food for Pregnancy by Lily Nichols

Spirit Babies by Walter Makichen

Super Nutrition for Babies by Katherine Erlich, M.D. and Kelly Genzlinger, M.Sc., C.N.C., C.M.T.A.

The Egg Quality Diet by Aimee E. Raupp

The Fertile Female by Julia Indichova

The Fifth Vital Sign by Lisa Hendrickson-Jack

MISCARRIAGE, INFERTILITY, REPRODUCTIVE IMMUNOLOGY, AND ENDOMETRIOSIS SUPPORT

selahfertility.com

pregmune.com

preventmiscarriage.com

theendometriosissummitt.com

resolve.org

REIKI AND BODY TALK

kittykatcoven.com

carolyngrace.org

FUNCTIONAL MEDICINE DOCTORS

Dr. Ben Lynch
drbenlynch.com/about/Kresser Institute

Kresser Institute
directory.chriskresser.com/practitioner-directory/?_ga=2.77219989.1261787140.1635191718-1066863040.1635191718

The Ultra Wellness Center
ultrawellnesscenter.com

The Institute for Functional Medicine
ifm.org/find-a-practitioner/

HEALTH FOOD DELIVERY SERVICES

Butcherbox
butcherbox.com

Thrive Market
thrivemarket.com

LABORATORIES

Reprosource
reprosource.com

Any Lab Test Now
anylabtestnow.com

Your Lab Work
yourlabwork.com/?ref=1585

NUTRITION

Lily Nichols, RDN
lilynicholsrdn.com

Jessica Ash, CNC, FDNP, HHC, CPT
jessicaashwellness.com

POSTPARTUM DEPRESSION

Postpartum Support International
postpartum.net

REPRODUCTIVE IMMUNOLOGISTS

Dr. Andrea Vidali/Braverman
Reproductive Immunology and Pregmune
preventmiscarriage.com
pregmune.com

Dr. Joanne Kwak-Kim of Rosalind Franklin University
Reproductive Medicine and Immunology/
University Health Clinics
rfuclinics.com/services/reproductivemedicineandimmunology/

Dr. Youseff Derbala of Derbala
Reproductive Immunology
derbalari.com

REPRODUCTIVE AND MATERNAL HEALTH THERAPY

Dr. Jessica Zucker
drjessicazucker.com/services

MENTAL HEALTH

Suicide and Crisis Hotline: 988

About the Author

I'm Laura Fletcher and I am a fighter and survivor. I gave birth to my first daughter in 2012 and, after surviving four earth-shattering, back-to-back miscarriages, to my second daughter in 2020. The grief of the miscarriages derailed my life and crippled me for years. I felt alone, angry, broken, and defective. I completely lost faith in myself, the medical system, and God.

When I started speaking out about my experience I realized, both to my elation and dismay, that I am far from alone. Almost every woman I know has faced fertility challenges, pregnancy complications, or miscarriage. The world, as a whole, needs a massive shift in how we approach fertility, pregnancy, and postpartum care. In 2020, I decided to become part of the solution by pursuing education to become certified as both a birth doula and a fertility doula. I received those certifications in 2022. In

2021 I founded Selah Fertility to address a deeply personal and deeply problematic occurrence in women's care: the commonality of "unexplained" miscarriage and infertility. Through Selah, I intend to leave no stone unturned in the pursuit of equipping individuals with the tools they need to optimize their health and, as an extension, their fertility.

I could not have made this journey without the love and support of my husband, Clay. When I met my Clay, I was a teenager. He was funny, kind, outgoing, talented, and fun. What I have learned as an adult, and as his wife, is that he is courageous, selfless, reliable, and the most loving man I've ever met. When Jolene was born, she was separated from me because she was so premature. My heart broke but I knew she'd be safe because Clay wouldn't leave her side. He held her for hours waiting for her to be released back to me. When Isla was born, she was taken to the NICU for CPAP support. Again my heart was broken and again I knew she would be safe. Clay watched over her until I was cleared to join them. When I called for an update from the room where I was recovering from my C-section, the nurse said, "Your husband is standing over her where he's been all night. I've worked in NICU for a long time, and I've never seen a dad do something like that before." As I say in the book, he's a keeper.